Global Perspectives
for Cambridge IGCSE®

Jo Lally

Oxford and Cambridge
leading education together

OXFORD
UNIVERSITY PRESS

OXFORD
UNIVERSITY PRESS

Great Clarendon Street, Oxford, OX2 6DP, United Kingdom

Oxford University Press is a department of the University of Oxford. It furthers the University's objective of excellence in research, scholarship, and education by publishing worldwide. Oxford is a registered trade mark of Oxford University Press in the UK and in certain other countries

British Library Cataloguing in Publication Data

Data available

978-0-19-839514-0

1 3 5 7 9 10 8 6 4 2

MIX
Paper from
responsible sources
FSC® C007785
FSC
www.fsc.org

Paper used in the production of this book is a natural, recyclable product made from wood grown in sustainable forests. The manufacturing process conforms to the environmental regulations of the country of origin.

Printed in Great Britain

Acknowledgements

® IGCSE is the registered trademark of Cambridge International Examinations.

The publisher would like to thank Cambridge International Examinations for their kind permission to reproduce the past paper question on p155. All other questions and all example answers, marks awarded and comments that appear in this book were written by the author. In examination, the way marks would be awarded to answers like these may be different. Cambridge International Examinations bears no responsibility for the example answers to test-style questions which are contained in this publication.

The author and publisher would like to thank Lauren Piebenga for her contribution as a consultant reviewer.

Cover image: PiyachatS/Shutterstock

p19: Monkey Business Images/Shutterstock; **p25**: Blickwinkel/Alamy; **p31**: Kuttig-People/Alamy; **p37**: Pete Niesen/Alamy; **p63**: Dr Morley Read/Shutterstock; **p69**: Jordi Delgado/Shutterstock; **p75**: Warmer/Shutterstock; **p81**: Smileus/Shutterstock; **p106**: University of Antwerp; **p107**: Lucas Vallecillos/Shutterstock; **p158**: T McCracken/ McHumour; **p198a**: David Hayward/Naked Pastor; **p198b**: Doug Savage; **p212**: Anthony Kelly/Cartoon Stock; **p216**: Chris Madden; **p175**: Polyp

Artwork by Q2A Media and Paul Hostetler

The author and publisher are grateful for permission to reprint extracts from the following copyright material:

Sally Adee: adapted excerpt from 'Zap your brain into the zone: Fast track to pure focus', 6 February 2012, *New Scientist*, © 2012 Reed Business Information – UK, all rights reserved, distributed by Tribune Content Agency, reprinted by permission.

Antislavery.org: excerpt from 'What is trafficking in people?', from www.antislavery.org, reprinted by permission.

Ian Birrell: excerpt from 'Corrupt, ineffective and hypocritical: Britain should give less aid, not more', 1 May 2013, *The Independent*, www.independent.co.uk, reprinted by permission.

Christian Aid: excerpts from 'Our work on trade', from www.christianaid.org.uk, © Christian Aid, reprinted by permission.

Common Sense Advisory: 'Figure 19.2: How non-Anglophone consumers use English-language websites', from 'Can't read, won't buy', Common Sense Advisory research, www.commonsenseadvisory.com, reprinted by permission.

Almuth Ernsting: excerpts adapted from 'Biomass: the Trojan horse of renewables?', 7 June 2013, www.redpepper.org.uk, reprinted by permission.

Giving What We Can: excerpt from 'Myths about aid', from www.givingwhatwecan.org, reprinted by permission.

INTERPOL: excerpt from 'Trafficking in human beings', from http://www.interpol.int, reprinted by permission.

Martin Luther King Jr.: excerpt from Acceptance Speech for The Nobel Peace Prize 1964, in Oslo, 10 December 1964 © The Nobel Foundation (1964), reprinted by permission.

Laura Klappenbach: excerpt from 'Things you can do to protect wildlife', © 2013 Laura Klappenback, from http://www.animals.about.com, reprinted by permission of About Inc., which can be found online at www.about.com, all rights reserved.

Sherryl Kleinman: excerpt from 'Why sexist language matters', from www.alternet.org, originally published in the *Center Line*, a newsletter of the Orange Country Rape Crisis Center, reprinted by permission.

Charles C. Mann: excerpts from 'What if we never run out of oil?', © 2013 The Atlantic Media Co., as first published in The Atlantic Magazine, all rights reserved, distributed by Tribune Content Agency, reprinted by permission.

NZ On Air: figure: 'Proportion of local content on prime-time television, 1988 – 2009', reprinted by permission.

Robyn Pennacchia: adapted excerpts from 'McDonalds' suggested budget for employees shows just how impossible it is to get by on minimum wage', 15 July 2013, from www.deathandtaxesmag.com, reprinted by permission.

United Nations Office on Drugs and Crime (UNODC): figure 'Gun murder compared by country (2004-2010), reprinted by permission.

World Bank: figure 'Map 0.1 Where financing comes first, inefficiencies are likely to

follow: Uncoordinated plans for housing and mass transport in Hanoi, Vietnam' and an excerpt from *Planning, Connecting, and Financing Cities* – Now © World Bank, http://hdl.handle.net/10986/12238, Licence: Creative Commons Attribution (CC BY 3.0 Unported licence)

Any third party use of this material, outside of this publication, is prohibited. Interested parties should apply to the copyright holders indicated in each case.

Although we have made every effort to trace and contact all copyright holders before publication this has not been possible in all cases. If notified, the publisher will rectify any errors or omissions at the earliest opportunity.

Links to third party websites are provided by Oxford in good faith and for information only. Oxford disclaims any responsibility for the materials contained in any third party website referenced in this work.

Contents

Introduction

Who is this book for?

This book is for:

- students studying Global Perspectives for Cambridge IGCSE®

- people who want to think independently about and debate important issues in the world

- anyone who wants to improve their thinking, reasoning, research, planning, teamwork and presentation skills.

How do I use this book?

This book is structured so that you can choose your own route through it – it's a sort of "build your own learning adventure" book.

The book has five sections, each a little bit more complex than the last. Section 1 introduces the skills and Section 5 develops them to a high level. Each section has:

- a **skills development chapter**. This will introduce, develop and help you practise the skills

- four **topic chapters** for you to choose from. These will help you to practise the skills and prepare for assessment.

It's best to work through the skills development chapters in order, rather than starting with Section 5. But going back to an earlier chapter to revise a skill can be a really good idea.

You can do as many of the topic chapters as you like – or as few. You may have to negotiate with your teacher to let you study a topic chapter you find interesting (rather than one your teacher finds interesting). Good luck – it will improve your presentation and reasoning skills! But be prepared to listen to your teacher too – listening is also an important skill in Global Perspectives. Furthermore, you have to choose the right moment to strike out independently. Your teacher just might have a valuable, informed opinion about whether you are ready for this. And you may be ready sooner, or later, than your classmates.

Every chapter guides you through the Global Perspectives learning process:

- Research information

- Question

- Reflect and plan

- Present your findings and act on them

At the beginning of each topic chapter there are suggested research questions and project outcomes. This will help you to understand what you are preparing for and why you are doing a particular task. As you progress through the course you will become more independent about setting your own questions and outcomes and planning your own research and activities.

It is also possible to work through some of the discussion points and activities in a topic chapter without completing the whole chapter or producing a research report and group project. You might, for example, want to discuss lots of issues a little bit before deciding on your individual research report and group project. Or you could work through one particular kind of skill (such as deciding whether consequences are likely or whether a text is logical) in several topic chapters to practise it until you are more confident.

In Sections 1 and 2 there are suggestions for mini research reports and projects. These are shorter and require less time to complete than assessed Global Perspectives Individual Research Reports and Group Projects. Doing at least one each of these will help you to practise the skills you need and to get feedback from your teacher, without the stress of knowing the result matters. If you enjoy these topics, you can talk to your teacher about how to adapt the mini research report and project to meet assessment criteria. In Sections 3, 4 and 5 the suggested research reports and group projects are full length and suitable for assessment.

In Sections 4 and 5 each topic chapter includes a practice written examination, similar to the assessed Written Examination. Those in Section 5 generally include more challenging questions to help students who are ready to really extend themselves.

What will I learn?

As you can see from the guidance on how to use this book, you will be able to choose – or at least negotiate with your teacher – quite a lot of what you learn. You will discuss and learn about a number of important global issues.

More importantly, however, you will develop, practise and apply the skills you need to research, plan and take action. You will learn to understand different perspectives on complex global issues, and you will learn to see the world differently.

Most importantly, we hope that you will learn that:

- you are not too young to think for yourself
- you are not too young to take action that really makes a difference
- you can change the future for your world.

Teacher guidance is available at www.oxfordsecondary.co.uk/gp

Section 1
Skills development activities

In this chapter, you will begin to develop the skills you need for Cambridge Global Perspectives™. The contexts for these skills will be taken from the following topics in Section 1:

- Family and demographic change
- Humans and other species
- Education for all
- Sport and recreation

The Global Perspectives learning process

Global Perspectives involves active learning. This means that you should be involved in every part of the course, from deciding what to study to finding your own information, thinking about the information and the issues, to carrying out an active project.

All the skills sections and topics in this handbook are structured around this learning process. It's a process with four main stages, and you will sometimes need to return to an earlier stage.

The diagram shows the stages in this active learning process.

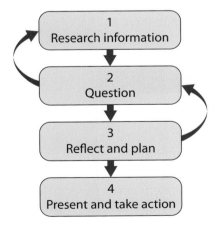

Figure 1 Global Perspectives is built around an active learning process

In all the topics, you will look at issues of global importance. You will be expected to show understanding of these global issues from personal, national and global perspectives.

Research information

In most of your other subjects, you probably learn information that the teacher gives you. In Global Perspectives, you will learn how to find and collect your own information. You will learn two main skills:

- How to identify what information you need
- How to collect and select information

Identifying what information you need

To start with, you will work with your teacher and your class to choose a topic, an issue, and a question about it. Deciding on a question will help you focus on a small part of the topic. Then you will think about the kind of information that will help you answer the question, and where to find that information. Let's look at an example:

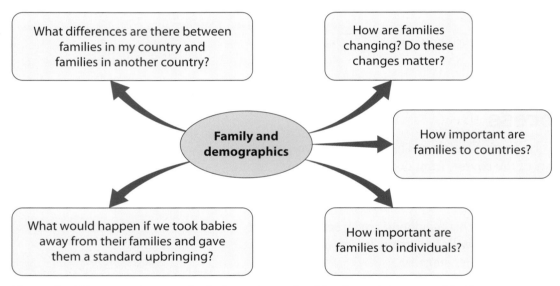

Figure 2a What questions can I ask about the topic of family and demographics?

One way of thinking about the kind of information you need is to have a class discussion and share ideas.

Activity 1

(a) Set some rules for class discussions. For example, one rule might be "We must listen to other people's ideas."

(b) "What differences are there between families in my country and families in another country?" Have a class discussion about the sort of information you need to find. What questions can help you?

(c) "What would happen if we took babies away from their families and gave them a standard upbringing?" Discuss what you think would happen. How is this question different from the question in (b)?

Figure 2b shows some more specific questions that will help us search for information and ideas.

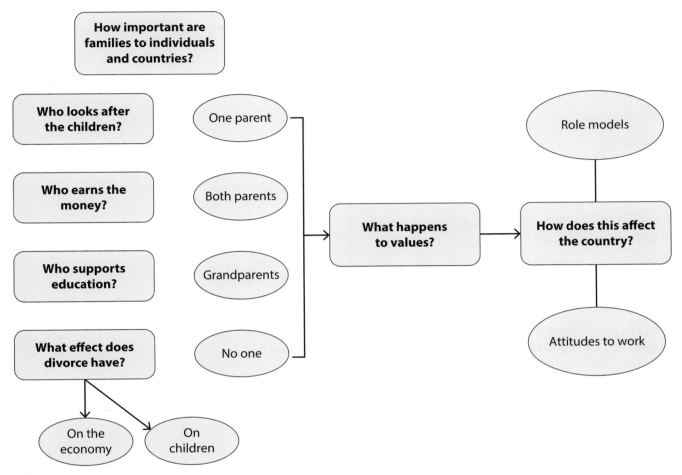

Figure 2b What information do I need?

Activity 2

(a) Choose one of the following questions about the topic of sport and recreation. Have a discussion in your class or group to decide what information you might need to help you answer it. You could draw a diagram or table to help you.

   (i)   What do national sports say about a country?

   (ii) Is sport just a "man thing"?

   (iii) Are darts, motor racing, and chess sports?

   (iv) Can international competitions help improve understanding between peoples?

(b) Choose from *either* humans and other species *or* education. Work in your group to break the topic down into smaller questions. Think about the sort of information you might need to help you answer the questions. Use diagrams or tables to help you.

What kind of answers do I need?

Before you do an Internet search for the answers, you need to think about the sort of answers, information, and ideas you need. They might be:

- definitions
- facts
- opinions
- value judgments
- predictions.

Let's look at some examples:

What is a family?

The answer to this question could be a definition. But it's not actually a very interesting question, is it?

What proportion of families are extended families?

A number or fact might answer this question. But then you have to ask some more questions: does extended mean with grandparents, aunts, uncles, or cousins? Is a family consisting of a grandmother, a mother, and a daughter an extended family or a single-parent family? How do we find out, from the millions of people in the country, what sort of families people live in? We can see that this question is not as simple as it seems.

How are families in China and the UK different from one another?

Some of the answers to this question are simple facts. For example, China has had a one-child policy for many years, so many Chinese children do not have brothers, sisters, aunts, or uncles. In the UK most children do have these relatives. In China, children are expected to obey and respect their parents. In the UK, most parents don't demand the same level of obedience and respect. But these simple facts don't really tell you much about the differences. What does it *feel* like not to have brothers or sisters? What effect does this have on family dynamics, people's behaviour, and the country? To answer this question properly, you need people's opinions and feelings as well as just the facts.

Why are families in China and the UK different from one another?

This question requires an explanation that deals with causes and consequences. Facts from history might explain some of the differences, but you have to consider how they link together as well.

Will changing divorce rates have a negative effect on the country?

First of all, this is a question about the future, so we don't have facts to answer this question. We have to make predictions. Secondly, this is a complex question. The answer depends on many things, such as welfare costs, the effects on children's education, and the effects on people's attitudes. Thirdly, it might be just a matter of opinion and value judgment whether these effects are positive or negative. For example, some people think that all children need two

parents, and others believe that one happy parent is better than two unhappy parents. Your opinion about this will change how you answer the question.

These examples show there are many different types of answers to questions. You'll look at them in more detail during the course. For now, you just need to think about getting the right *kind* of answer to your questions. A definition or a simple fact will not answer a complicated question.

Activity 3

What sort of answers do you need for the following questions?

(a) What is a national sport?

(b) What is the national sport of Bhutan?

(c) What is education? (Think carefully about this one – is it really a simple definition?)

(d) Why is education necessary?

(e) What would be the best sort of education?

(f) What other species live in your country?

(g) Why does it matter if a species becomes extinct?

> You'll think about the answers to these questions later. For now, just think about what kinds of question they are and the sorts of answer they will need.

Finding the answers

Internet search terms

You have now thought about what sort of information you want. This will help you structure your Internet search to find this information.

- Be precise.
- Target your search terms to what you want to know.
- Add the name of a country, e.g. "family values + Singapore" or "family values + USA".
- Change your search terms if necessary.
- Look at the titles of the pages you find. Do they look as if they will answer your questions? If not, change your search terms.

> You don't have to read a page or site if it doesn't look useful.

Activity 4

In this activity, do not read the text on the sites you find. Scan the pages quickly to decide whether you think they will help you answer the questions in Figures 2a and 2b.

(a) Put "family" into your search engine. What sort of sites do you find?

(b) Put "family values" into your search engine. What sort of sites do you find?

(c) Put "effect divorce family values" into your search engine. What sort of sites do you find?

(d) Discuss in class which of these sites you expect to be more helpful in answering the questions in Figures 2a and 2b. How did you make this judgment?

Identifying useful information and ideas

In Activity 4 you should have discovered that the more precise your search terms are, the more useful your results will be. Now you need to think about how to find the information and ideas you need.

● Think about the kind of information you want, and the kind of information on the sites you are finding. Do they match? If not, move on.

● Go beyond the first site you find – even past the first page of search results!

● Use the information you find to help you search further.

For example, if your question is "Do family values matter as much in the UK as in China?" you search for "family values" and find **http://en.wikipedia.org/wiki/Family_values**

Does the information on this site match the kind of answer you need? Not really. This site gives you some facts, but it doesn't explain them, debate them or provide values or opinions. However, it can give you a starting point. Now you might decide you want to learn more about Confucian family values. You can change your search and look for "Confucian family values" or "importance of family values UK China" or "why do family values matter?"

Activity 5

(a) Which of the following sets of search terms would best help you answer the question, "Who cares for the children (parents, mothers, or grandparents, etc)?"

(i) "Who cares for children?"

(ii) "Caregiver"

(iii) Family structure + country

(iv) Men women childcare

Remember, there isn't "an answer" to most of these questions. What you are trying to do is find out enough information to form a reasonable opinion.

(b) What search terms would help you find information and ideas to answer these questions?

(i) How are humans causing extinction?

(ii) Does it matter if some species become extinct?

(iii) How can we prevent species extinction?

(iv) Do the Olympic Games successfully create peace?

(v) Is it all right for sports people to use drugs to improve their sporting performance?

(vi) Is it possible to have a truly fair sports competition between nations?

Skim reading

When you are looking for and selecting useful information, you do not have to read the whole of an article. You only need to skim read it to see if it is relevant. If it does seem relevant, you can then read it in more detail. Here is how to skim read:

1. Look for key words.

2. When you find the key words, read the sentence that they are in to see if it is relevant.

3. Read for gist – ask yourself what the article or paragraph is about.

4. Don't worry if you don't know some of the words; you can probably understand enough without them. At this stage, only look up words if you really need to.

Activity 6

(a) For each of these questions, decide which key words to look for.

   (i) Are single-parent families a recent change to family structures?

   (ii) Is it possible to have a truly fair sports competition between nations?

   (iii) How can we prevent species extinction?

(b) Skim read each of the following paragraphs, looking for key words and reading for gist. Will any of them help to answer the questions in **(a)**?

   (i) International sport is fundamentally not fair. Rich nations can afford to spend more resources on finding and training elite sports people than poor nations. This inevitably means that they have an advantage in international sporting competitions.

   (ii) People attack single mothers because they believe that unmarried mothers are living on welfare, have too many children and don't want to work. They also believe that single mothers will destroy family values. Yet half of US mothers on welfare were married but are now divorced. Furthermore, a woman can pass on good values to her children, even if their father left or died.

   (iii) Perhaps the greatest threat that faces many species is the widespread destruction of habitat. Deforestation, farming, overgrazing and development all result in irreversible changes such as soil compaction, erosion, desertification, or the alteration of local climatic conditions. Such land-use practices vastly alter or even eliminate wildlife habitat. In areas where rare species are present, habitat destruction can quickly force a species to extinction. We therefore need to find ways of protecting these wildlife habitats.

   (iv) During slavery, children stayed with their mothers when their fathers were sold, so women tended to be the head of their family. During the decades after slavery, single-mother families continued to be formed because of hard economic times, men being killed and men and women moving to look for work. Between 1880 and 1895, single mothers headed about 30 per cent of urban black families in the US.

   (v) There is a new trend in youth sports – sideline fights involving parents. Some of these are just petty, but increasingly, they are serious. A brawl between fathers at a youth hockey game in Massachusetts led to a death. A father in Texas shot and wounded the head coach at a high school football game. A father in Toronto tried to choke the hockey coach because his 8 year old son had been left out of the team for missing practices.

> Do not use a dictionary for part **(b)**.

Source: http://www.thedailygreen.com/environmental-news/latest/extinction-tips-47051605

Question

Once you've decided what you need to know and started to find some information and ideas, you need to start thinking about and questioning the information and ideas you have found.

Facts, opinions, predictions and value judgments

As mentioned earlier, you need different kinds of information and ideas to answer your questions. Four really important kinds are:

- facts
- opinions
- predictions
- value judgments.

Facts are pieces of information that are true. You can *verify* a fact – that is, you can find out whether it is true or not. For example, the statement "It is raining" might be a fact – or it might be false. You can check by looking outside.

Opinions are beliefs, views, or judgments. They are things that people think that are not necessarily true or factual. For example, the statement "Peas taste disgusting" is a matter of opinion, which varies from person to person. You can disagree with an opinion but you can't check whether or not it is true.

Predictions are attempts to foresee or say what will happen in the future. For example, the statement "It will rain tomorrow" is a prediction, and we can't tell whether it is an accurate one yet. However, we can think about how likely or unlikely a prediction is to happen.

Value judgments are a particular kind of opinion. They deal with values about what is good and bad, right and wrong. One example of a value judgment is "It is wrong for children to grow up without a father." We can't check whether value judgments are true, but we can think about whether they are reasonable and whether we accept them (and why).

Activity 7

Are the following statements facts, opinions, predictions, or value judgments? Explain why.

(a) There have been single-parent families for a long time.

(b) Single-parent families can be just as good for children as two-parent families.

(c) Sport should be fair.

(d) There are 11 people on a cricket team.

(e) It's selfish and greedy of humans to destroy natural habitats.

(f) Fighting shouldn't be part of the Olympic Games.

(g) Education is the most important part of a child's life.

(h) Brazil will win the football World Cup next year.

Disagreeing with opinions

An important part of Global Perspectives is having discussions and really thinking about different opinions. This means thinking about your own opinions and being prepared to change them. You can ask yourself the following questions:

- Have I got good reasons for my opinion?

- Is my opinion based on facts and thinking?

- Is my opinion based on emotion or ignorance?

You can ask the same questions about someone else's opinion. You can also ask yourself:

- Do I agree with this opinion?

- If so, why do I agree with this opinion?

- If not, why do I disagree with this opinion?

> Remember to respect your partner even if you disagree with their opinion.

Activity 8

(a) Give reasons why you agree or disagree with each of the following opinions.

(i) Family is more important than friends.

(ii) Sport is boring.

(iii) Everyone should stay at school until they are 18.

(iv) There is no point recycling things.

(b) Work with a partner who disagrees with you and discuss your reasons.

(i) Listen to what your partner is saying.

(ii) Really think about what your partner is saying.

(iii) Really examine why you think what you think.

(iv) Would finding more information help? If so, what sort of information?

(v) Can you find a compromise? If not, why not?

Identifying causes and consequences

A **cause** makes something happen. A **consequence** happens because of something else – it is a result or effect. We see causes and consequences in everyday life.

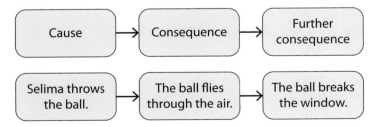

Figure 3a A simple cause and its consequences

In this example, Selima did not intend to break the window, but she did cause the window to break. The ball only moves because Selima throws it.

Selima's throw is the cause of the ball's movement, and the ball's movement is the cause of the broken window.

This seems like a simple chain of cause and consequence. However, the reality is more complex:

Selima's mother, Dr Khan, sees only a broken window and a ball. Dr Khan does not know that Selima's friend has stolen her phone. Dr Khan does know that Selima's brother Imran is cricket mad, and Selima thinks ball games are stupid. So Dr Khan believes that Imran threw the ball. She shouts at Imran and tells him he's a bad boy. Imran thinks this is unreasonable so he puts a frog in Selima's bed.

Can we say that Selima's friend caused Imran to put a frog in Selima's bed? There is a chain of causes. But these two events are quite a long way apart in that chain. We also need to consider Dr Khan's mistaken belief and the way Imran's mind works.

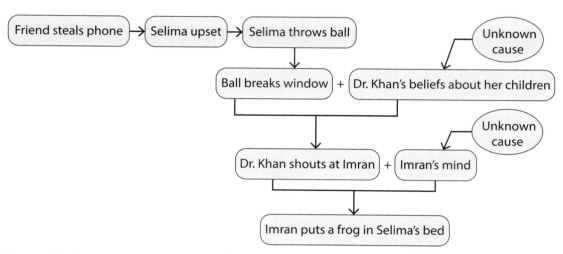

Figure 3b The more complex chain of events

We don't know what caused Dr Khan's beliefs about her children, or why Imran thinks putting a frog in his sister's bed is a good idea. We also don't know what caused Selima's friend to steal her phone. We can now see that what seemed like a simple cause and consequences is actually quite complex.

The relationship between causes and consequences can become even more complex in the issues we deal with in the Global Perspectives course. Sometimes a cause can have several consequences, some good and some bad, as in the following example.

Ari and Harjanti Budiman are poor but have high hopes for their children, Ridwan and Liana. Ari is offered a government contract logging in the rainforest. He thinks that cutting down ancient trees is wrong but the money allows him to send Ridwan and Liana to school. Ridwan and Liana do well at school, and eventually get good jobs with good money. But logging in the rainforest has caused habitat loss and species extinction.

> Words that help to identify causes: because, as, since
>
> Words that help to identify consequences: so, therefore, that's why, as a result

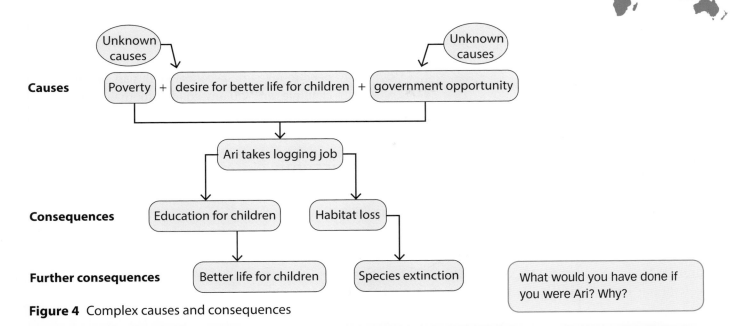

Causes

Unknown causes → Poverty + desire for better life for children + government opportunity ← Unknown causes

Ari takes logging job

Consequences

Education for children   Habitat loss

Further consequences

Better life for children   Species extinction

What would you have done if you were Ari? Why?

Figure 4 Complex causes and consequences

Activity 9

(a) Identify the causes and consequences in the following. Draw diagrams if it helps you.

- **(i)** Rich nations do better in international sporting events than poor nations because they can afford to find, develop, and train elite athletes.

- **(ii)** Frank got a bad mark in his maths exam. So he believed he was bad at maths. So he stopped trying. So he became bad at maths. So when Frank opened his own business, he made a mess of the accounts. So his business failed.

- **(iii)** Ilke got a bad mark in her maths exam. So she worked hard for her next maths exam. So she got a better mark. So she realized that hard work could lead to success.

- **(iv)** Deforestation, farming, overgrazing and development all result in irreversible changes such as soil compaction, erosion, desertification, or the alteration of local climatic conditions. Such land-use practices lead to habitat loss.

- **(v)** People are living longer lives than they used to. They are also having fewer children. This means that a small number of adults are providing for a large number of older people.

(b) Imran put a frog in Selima's bed. What could be the consequences of this action, in your opinion?

(c) What do you think caused the following events? Do you think the causes are simple or complex? Discuss the possibilities in groups.

- **(i)** Jasper got a bad mark in his maths test.
- **(ii)** Khalila got a detention.
- **(iii)** Santiago's parents got a divorce.
- **(iv)** Emily's grandparents came to live with her and her family.
- **(v)** Brazil did not win the football World Cup.

(d) How would you try to find out the real causes of the action in **(b)**?

(e) What might be the consequences of the following events? Discuss the possibilities in groups.

- **(i)** Petra says to the teacher, "Can you stop saying the same things over and over again and actually do something interesting, please?"
- **(ii)** You trial for your national football team.
- **(iii)** You work really hard at school for the next two years.

(iv) You spend more time doing household chores with your parents.

(v) Your grandparents come to live with you.

(f) Are some of the consequences you think of more likely than others? What other factors would you need to take into account? With part **(e)** **(ii)**, for example, are you any good at football, and how will this affect the consequences?

Personal, national, and global perspectives

Most actions and events can be seen from personal, national, and global perspectives. Even personal choices can be part of the cause of global events.

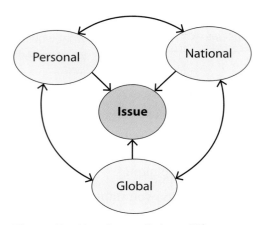

Figure 5a How issues link to different perspectives

For every question set on this course, we can think of personal and national as well as global perspectives. Look at the question, "Should education be free for all?" for example.

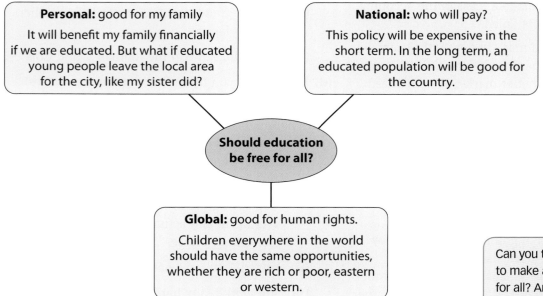

Personal: good for my family

It will benefit my family financially if we are educated. But what if educated young people leave the local area for the city, like my sister did?

National: who will pay?

This policy will be expensive in the short term. In the long term, an educated population will be good for the country.

Should education be free for all?

Global: good for human rights.

Children everywhere in the world should have the same opportunities, whether they are rich or poor, eastern or western.

Can you think of any more points to make about free education for all? Are your points personal, national or global?

Figure 5b Perspectives on an issue

Activity 10

Think of personal, national and global perspectives on these questions. You can think of points, questions, causes, or consequences. Draw diagrams to help you.

(i) Should I go to my training for the national Judo team tonight or revise for my exam?

(ii) Should the government give extra money to married couples?

(iii) Is it right to eat meat from animals that have been kept in poor conditions?

(iv) Should the country refuse to import wood from cleared rainforest?

(v) Should parents encourage their children to train hard at a sport?

Reflect and plan

You've researched some information and started to question it. Now you need to reflect on the ideas and issues contained in the information, and try to decide what you really think about it. You can also start to plan any action you could take.

What is more important?

In many of the issues you will discuss on the course, there will be hard decisions to make. When you are reflecting, you can think about the relative importance of different things. For example, is sending children to school more important than protecting rainforest habitats and species? Does your opinion change if your perspective changes? Does it make a difference if they are *your* children? There are many children in the world, but fewer than 60 Javan rhinoceroses (which live in threatened habitats in Indonesia). Does this make a difference?

There are no "right" answers. Reflection is about knowing what you think, and why you think that way.

Activity 11

(a) In each case below, say which option would be more important to you, and why. Does your view change if your perspective changes?

    (i) Keeping your parents happy or following your dream?

    (ii) Playing for the national team or getting good grades?

    (iii) Staying married even though you argue, or divorcing in the hope of happiness?

    (iv) Happiness or wealth?

    (v) Success for your family, success for your nation, or success for your favourite sports team?

(b) Think of some of the other issues you've discussed in this skills section. What aspects of them do you think are most important, and why?

Forming and changing opinions

Reflection can be about forming opinions on issues you hadn't thought about before. It can also mean changing your mind in response to your thinking.

Setting an outcome

In Global Perspectives you don't collect information just because it's nice to have information. You collect information and ideas for a purpose. That purpose can be to make a decision, to recommend a course of action, or to take action.

During the course you may complete one or more small projects in which you and your group practise how to plan and take action. You will complete a project for your final assessment.

The first key task, when you are planning a project, is to set an outcome. This means deciding what action to take. Your action needs to be SMART:

Activity 12

(a) Have you formed any new opinions so far? Give examples and say why.

(b) Have you changed your mind about any issues? Give examples and say why.

Specific

Measurable

Achievable

Realistic

Time-bound

Don't underestimate what you can do. Be ambitious – but be realistic.

Figure 6 SMART outcomes

Let's look at two different outcomes and see whether they are SMART.

	A: Outcome: end world poverty	B: Outcome: design and make a set of T-shirts promoting family values to sell at the school open day.
Specific?	No: ending world poverty is quite a broad, vague aim.	Yes.
Measurable?	No: how would you tell if you'd achieved this? (What is poverty? How do we measure it?)	Yes.
Achievable?	No. You'd probably have to be a superhero to end world poverty on a Saturday afternoon between finishing your maths homework and starting your English.	Yes, this is possible (unless the school open day is tomorrow).
Realistic?	No.	Yes. This is a project that is realistic for young people with limited time.
Time-bound?	No.	Yes. There is a clear deadline.

Activity 13

(a) Look at the following list of outcomes. Are they SMART for a group of 14–16-year-olds doing a school project?

   (i) Passing a law to ban divorce.

   (ii) Producing a short video showing the negative effects of divorce on children.

   (iii) Finding a solution to habitat destruction.

   (iv) Writing and performing a song about species extinction to sing at a school event.

   (v) Volunteering once a week with a local sports charity to help disabled children gain confidence.

(b) Think of an action you'd like to take in each of the following topic areas. Is it a SMART outcome for a school project?

   (i) Family and demographics

   (ii) Humans and other species

   (iii) Education

   (iv) Sport and recreation

> When you actually decide on a project outcome, you will have done much more research and thinking!

Teamwork and leadership

You will work in a team during the Global Perspectives course as you work on a group project. This requires different skills from those you need when you work on your own, doing homework, individual research, or learning for the exam. You will need to trust and co-operate with your team members.

Activity 14

(a) The teacher will plan a route through your school. You will work in groups of three. One person will be blindfolded. One person will have a map of the route but will not be able to speak. One person will be able to speak, but will not be allowed to look at the map. The blindfolded person must arrive safely at the end of the route.

What issues of teamwork does this exercise raise?

(b) Work in teams of three to five. You will need drinking straws, sticky tape, and a plastic cup full of water. You have 15 minutes to build a structure that will support the cup of water.

   (i) Which team was most effective? Why was this? How did their team work?

   (ii) How important were thinking and planning?

   (iii) What happens if no one takes the lead or makes decisions?

   (iv) What happens if everyone wants to make decisions?

Present and take action

The final stages of the Global Perspectives learning process are presenting ideas and information and taking the action you have planned. Your presentation must always have a purpose, which might be to express an opinion and give your reasons for it, or to answer a question. You will never need just to list information you have found.

Communicate in clear English

It is extremely important to communicate in clear English.

- Use your own words.
- Use clear, simple sentences.
- Communicating ideas is more important than grammatical accuracy, but mistakes matter if they make your meaning unclear.

Expressing opinions and giving reasons

We have already talked about expressing opinions and giving reasons for them. This is really important when you are presenting your ideas or persuading people to support your decision.

Let's look at an example.

Opinion: I believe that it is good for extended families to live together.

Reasons: You can all support each other. There is always someone around who has time for the children. You don't get lonely.

When you are presenting, you can use words like *because, so, therefore, also, in addition*. These words help you to show the links between your ideas. For example:

I believe that it is good for extended families to live together **because** you can all support each other. **Also**, there is always someone around who has time for the children, **so** we don't get lonely.

You can also add examples to illustrate your point. For example:

I believe that it is good for extended families to live together **because** you can all support each other. **Also**, there is always someone around who has time for the children, **so** we don't get lonely. **For example,** when my parents are at work, my grandmother often spends time baking with my brother and me.

Activity 15

(a) Connect the following sentences using *because, so, therefore, also, in addition* and *for example*. Think about which part is the opinion and which parts are the reasons and examples.

(i) Ari Budiman is right to take the logging job. Education for his children is the most important thing. If work is hard to find, you take what you can get.

(ii) International sports competitions put different nations in opposition to each other. It is like a mini war. You are happy when the other country loses. You believe that your country winning is most important. During the Olympics, I really wanted the competitor from my country to win, even though the other competitor was better. International sports competitions actually make us less peaceful.

(b) Answer the following questions by giving your opinion. Give reasons and examples.

(i) Do we have the right to use animals however we like?

(ii) Should children always do what their parents want?

(iii) Are some children better off working than being at school?

(iv) Should we have less sport on national television?

There are four chapters next that deal with topics from the Cambridge Global Perspectives™ syllabus. You do not need to work through them all! You should work through the activities in at least one of the topics for this section. It would be useful for you to try a "mini" research report. Ideas are suggested for "mini" projects to help you get used to working in teams and producing an outcome.

Remember that you can select just some activities from all of the topics in this section if you need to practise a particular skill. For example, Activities 1.2, 2.2, 3.2 and 4.2 all help you to think about the kind of information you need to answer a question.

Section 1

1 Family and demographic change

Figure 1.1 People live in many types of family group

In this chapter, you are going to work through the Global Perspectives learning process. As described in the skills development activities on pages 1–17, this process involves taking the following steps:

1. Research information

2. Question

3. Reflect and plan

4. Present and take action

You are going to go through this process as you prepare for and complete a short practice individual research report and a mini group project on the topic. You will also be practising and using the skills you started to learn in the skills development activities for this section.

Research information

By following the steps in this chapter, you'll develop the skills that will enable you to produce two good pieces of work: a research report and a project. First, you will need to choose one research question and one project from the lists in the box above Activity 1.1 and then research relevant information.

Suggested mini research questions and mini project outcomes

(a) Choose one of these research questions.

   (i) How should societies deal with the problems of older people?

   (ii) What are the best solutions to the problems of managing work and family life?

   (iii) How should families change to deal with the challenges of the 21st century?

(b) Choose one of these project outcomes.

   (i) Make a photo display of families. Working with a team from a different country or culture (your teacher can help you organize this), share photos of your families. Discuss differences in family structure and family values.

   (ii) Design a poster explaining the value of families.

   (iii) Use one of the ideas from Activity 13 in the skills development activities on page 15, for your project.

> If you are choosing your own project, remember to set a SMART outcome.

Activity 1.1

Think about which research questions or project outcome you would like to try from the box above. You can use the next few activities to help you research, think and decide.

What information do I need?

To answer your research question, you'll need to work out what information you need. For example, for the suggested research question listed in part **(a) (i)** above, you might ask:

- What are the problems of older people?
- What causes these problems?
- What are the consequences of these problems?

You should also think about the *kind* of information you need. This might be definitions, facts, opinions, value judgments, or predictions (see page 8).

Activity 1.2

(a) What kind of information do you need to answer each of the following questions?

    (i) What are demographics?

    (ii) How many older people live alone?

    (iii) Will men soon be as involved in childcare as women are?

    (iv) Who should look after older people?

    (v) What is the average life expectancy in your country?

    (vi) Is a nuclear family better than an extended family?

(b) Work in a group with other people who are interested in the same research question as you. Discuss the following questions, and draw diagrams or use tables to note your ideas.

    (i) What questions should you ask to help you find information?

    (ii) What kind of information will help you answer each of your questions?

> Remember your class rules about discussions.

Finding information

To find information, you need to:

- use the right search terms (see page 5)
- skim-read long documents, looking for key words (see page 6)
- read small parts of documents for detail (see page 6).

Activity 1.3

(a) What search terms will help you find information and ideas to answer these questions?

    (i) Is a nuclear family better than an extended family?

    (ii) How are families changing in your country?

    (iii) How are families changing in another country?

    (iv) What are the problems faced by working parents?

(b) What search terms will help you answer the questions in part **(a)** of Activity 1.2?

(c) What key words will you look for in documents when you start to search for information?

> If you can't find the information you need, change your search terms.

Question

Once you have found a piece of information, always ask yourself the following questions about it:

- Is this a fact, an opinion, a prediction, or a value judgment?
- Do I agree with the opinions given?
- What are the causes and consequences here?
- What are its personal, national and global perspectives?

Activity 1.4

Anya: "My family are wonderful and annoying. They are always there when I need them, but they never let me do what I want. My parents are both teachers. I'm the eldest child, and I've got three little sisters and a little brother. All four of my grandparents live with us. My mother's mother and my father's mother don't like each other, so they are always arguing, about *everything*."

Kofi: "I live with my Mum. It's just the two of us. Sometimes this is great, because we watch films together and cook together. I help with the household chores – it's only fair, because I make a mess too. Sometimes, though, I wish we had a bigger family. I think my mum will be lonely when I leave home."

(a) Anya says, "They never let me do what I want." Is this a fact or an opinion? Explain your answer.

(b) Identify one fact, one opinion, one prediction, and one value judgment in Kofi's words. Explain your answers.

(c) What do you think are the causes of Anya's big family living together?

(d) What do you think will be the consequences of Anya's big family living together?

(e) What might be the consequences if your whole family lived together?

(f) What do you think are the causes of Kofi's small family?

(g) What do you think will be the consequences of Kofi's small family?

(h) What might be the consequences if you lived alone with just one other family member?

(i) Which is better, in your opinion – a big family or a small family? Give reasons for your answer.

(j) From a national perspective, are big families or small families better? Give reasons for your answer.

Activity 1.5

(a) Make a final choice of research questions for your individual research. Use the skills you have been practising to help you to research ideas, information and perspectives.

(b) Look through your research materials for your individual research.

(i) Make sure you know when you are reading facts, opinions, predictions, and value judgments.

(ii) Think about which opinions you agree with, and which you don't. Work in a group to discuss the opinions.

(iii) Draw diagrams and tables to show the causes and consequences in the issue you've chosen.

(iv) Draw diagrams to help you think about the personal, national and global perspectives.

(v) Do you need to find any more information? What else do you need to know?

Remember to respect other people's opinions even when you don't agree with them.

Reflect and plan

Take some time to think about the information, ideas, issues, and perspectives that you have been researching. At this stage you can also start to plan your group project.

Activity 1.6

(a) You should now have thought about families in some new ways. Think about what you have learned and why this might broaden your perspective.

(b) Have you changed your mind about anything? If so, in what way? If not, why not?

Work in groups to discuss parts (c) to (f). Afterwards, let the different ideas and opinions float around in your mind for a few days. Keep thinking about them.

(c) In families, which of these do you think is more important, and why?

    (i)   Support or independence? (Does it make a difference if you're young or old?)

    (ii) Love or money?

    (iii) Closeness or distance?

(d) How much pressure should parents place on their children to succeed? Explain your opinion.

(e) How much obedience should parents expect from their children? Explain your opinion.

(f) How far should parents set goals for their children? How far should children be able to set their own life aims? Explain your opinion.

> Do you have to choose between support or independence, love or money, closeness or distance? How can you find the right balance?

Activity 1.7

Work in teams to decide on and plan your project.

(a) Agree on a project outcome.

(b) Decide on team roles, for example who will be the leader.

(c) Copy and complete the table.

Task	Who will do it	When it should be done
1		
2		
3		
4		

> Make your table as long as it needs to be for all the tasks.

Present and act

You have now had time to reflect on the information, ideas, issues, and perspectives for your research report.

Activity 1.8

Write a research report of 300–500 words on your chosen question. Use these headings:

- The problem
- The causes of the problem
- The consequences
- Personal, national, and global perspectives
- The possible solution
  (give your opinions here to answer the question)

Activity 1.9

Carry out your group project. Then answer these questions:

(a) How well did your team work together?

(b) What problems did you have?

(c) How did you solve these problems?

(d) How will you avoid these problems next time?

Section 1
2 Humans and other species

Figure 2.1 How does human activity affect other species?

In this chapter, you are going to work through the Global Perspectives learning process. As described in the skills development activities on pages 1–17, this process involves taking the following steps:

1. Research information

2. Question

3. Reflect and plan

4. Present and take action

You are going to go through this process as you prepare for and complete a short practice individual research report and a mini group project on the topic. You will also be practising and using the skills you started to learn in the skills development activities for this section.

Research information

By following the steps in this chapter, you'll develop the skills that will enable you to produce two good pieces of work: a research report and a group project. First, you will need to choose one research question and one project from the lists in the box above Activity 2.1 and then research relevant information.

Suggested mini research questions and mini project outcomes

(a) Choose one of these research questions.

    (i) How can individuals and nations help reduce habitat destruction?

    (ii) How can we improve the ways in which we treat animals in our country?

    (iii) How can we prevent the hunting of endangered species?

(b) Choose one of these project outcomes.

    (i) Make a photo display of endangered species. Explain why species extinction matters.

    (ii) Produce a public service advertisement to show actions we can all take to reduce the impact of our lifestyle on other species.

    (iii) Use one of the ideas from Activity 13 in the skills development activities on page 15, for your project.

Activity 2.1

Think about which research questions or project outcome you would like to try from the box above. You can use the next few activities to help you research, think and decide.

> If you are choosing your own project, remember to set a SMART outcome.

What information do I need?

To answer your research question, you'll need to work out what information you need. For example, for the suggested research question listed in part **(a) (ii)** above, you might ask:

- What are the problems in the way we treat animals?
- What causes these problems?
- What are the consequences of these problems?

You should also think about the *kind* of information you need. This might be definitions, facts, opinions, value judgments, or predictions (see page 8).

Activity 2.2

(a) What kind of information do you need to answer each of these questions?

    (i) What is habitat destruction?

    (ii) What proportion of people in your country are vegetarian?

    (iii) What would happen if we all stopped eating meat?

    (iv) Why should we respect the other creatures on this planet?

    (v) How many different species live in Brunei's Sungai Ingei Conservation Forest?

    (vi) Why do Indonesian rainforests matter?

(b) Work in a group with other people who are interested in the same research question as you. Discuss the following questions, and draw diagrams or use tables to note your ideas.

    (i) What questions should you ask to help you find information?

    (ii) What kind of information will help you answer each of your questions?

> Remember your class rules about discussions.

Finding information

To find information, you need to:

- use the right search terms (see page 5)
- skim-read long documents, looking for key words (see page 6)
- read small parts of documents for detail (see page 6).

Activity 2.3

(a) What search terms will help you find information and ideas to answer these questions?

    (a) What proportion of people in your country are vegetarian?

    (b) What would happen if we all stopped eating meat?

    (c) How many different species live in Brunei's Sungai Ingei Conservation Forest?

    (d) Why do Indonesian rainforests matter?

(b) What search terms will help you answer the questions you identified in part **(b) (i)** of Activity 2.2?

(c) What key words will you look for in documents when you start to search for information?

> Do you need to use the Internet to answer all these questions? How else could you find out this information?

> If you can't find the information you need, change your search terms.

Question

Once you have found a piece of information, always ask yourself the following questions about it:

- Is this a fact, an opinion, a prediction, or a value judgment?
- Do I agree with the opinions given?
- What are the causes and consequences here?
- What are its personal, national and global perspectives?

Activity 2.4

Keith: "We should all become vegetarians. If we did, there would be enough food for everyone. It takes 7 kg of grain to produce 1 kg of beef. It also takes thousands and thousands of litres of water. Also, it's wrong to eat beef. It's murder."

Jacquie: "People are so bad at using statistics. It takes 7 kg of grain to produce 1 kg of beef on intensive US farms. But around the world, most beef is grass fed, and the grass grows on land that isn't good enough for grain production. I wouldn't eat beef from cows that had been kept in poor conditions, but it's not wrong to eat meat – it's a natural part of who we are."

(a) Keith says, "We should all become vegetarians." Is this a fact or an opinion? Explain your answer.

(b) Identify one fact, one prediction, and one value judgment that Keith uses. Explain your answers.

(c) Jacquie says, "…the grass grows on land that isn't good enough for grain production." Is this a fact or an opinion? Explain your answer.

(d) What might be the personal consequences for you of not eating meat?

(e) What might be the national and global consequences if no one ate meat?

(f) Large tracts of rainforest in South America are cut down to graze beef cattle and grow soya to feed crops.

   (i) What consequences might this have?

   (ii) How does this fact affect your opinion about eating beef?

Is natural the same as right? Is unnatural the same as wrong? Discuss this!

Activity 2.5

(a) Make a final choice of research questions for your individual research. Use the skills you have been practising to help you to research ideas, information and perspectives.

(b) Look through your research materials for your individual research.

   (i) Make sure you know when you are reading facts, opinions, predictions, and value judgments.

   (ii) Think about which opinions you agree with, and which you don't. Work in a group to discuss the opinions.

   (iii) Draw diagrams and tables to show the causes and consequences in the issue you've chosen.

   (iv) Draw diagrams to help you think about the personal, national and global perspectives.

   (v) Do you need to find any more information? What else do you need to know?

Remember to respect other people's opinions even when you don't agree with them.

Reflect and plan

Take some time to think about the information, ideas, issues, and perspectives that you have been researching. At this stage you can also start to plan your group project.

Activity 2.6

(a) You should now have thought about humans and other species in some new ways. Think about what you have learned and why this might broaden your perspective.

(b) Have you changed your mind about anything? If so, in what way? If not, why not?

Work in groups to discuss questions (c) to (f). Afterwards, let the different ideas and opinions float around in your mind for a few days. Keep thinking about them.

(c) Which of these do you think is more important, and why?

   (i)   Animal rights or benefits for humans?

   (ii) Good conditions for animals or cheap meat for humans?

   (iii) Economic development for humans or healthy natural habitats?

(d) Would the world be a better place if we reduced the number of humans? Explain your opinion.

(e) How much do endangered species matter to you/to the world? Explain your opinion.

(f) Is it selfish to protect endangered species for our own benefit? Explain your opinion.

Activity 2.7

Work in teams to decide on and plan your project.

(a) Agree on a project outcome.

(b) Decide on team roles, for example who will be the leader.

(c) Copy and complete the table.

Task	Who will do it	When it should be done

> Make your table as long as it needs to be for all the tasks.

Present and take action

You have now had time to reflect on the information, ideas, issues, and perspectives for your research report.

Activity 2.8

Write a research report of 300–500 words on your chosen question. Use these headings:

- The problem

- The causes of the problem

- The consequences

- Personal, national, and global perspectives

- The possible solution
  (give your opinions here to answer the question)

Activity 2.9

Carry out your group project. Then answer these questions:

(a) How well did your team work together?

(b) What problems did you have?

(c) How did you solve these problems?

(d) How will you avoid these problems next time?

Section 1
3 Education for all

How is your Global Perspectives classroom different from the classroom in this picture? How important do you think these differences are to your education?

Figure 3.1 What is the value of education?

In this chapter, you are going to work through the Global Perspectives learning process. As described in the skills development activities on pages 1–17, this process involves taking the following steps:

1. Research information

2. Question

3. Reflect and plan

4. Present and take action

You are going to go through this process as you prepare for and complete a short practice individual research report and a mini group project on the topic. You will also be practising and using the skills you started to learn in the skills development activities for this section.

Research information

By following the steps in this chapter, you'll develop the skills that will enable you to produce two good pieces of work: a research report and a group project. You will need to choose one research question and one project from the lists in the box above Activity 3.1 and then research relevant information.

Suggested mini research questions and mini project outcomes

(a) Choose one of these research questions.

   (i)   How should we deal with the problems in our education system?

   (ii) Should education be free for all? If so, what steps can we take to achieve this?

   (iii) How can we ensure that young people understand the value of education?

(b) Choose one of these project outcomes.

   (i)   Make a photo display showing the differences between your school and a school in a different country or culture. Work with a team in a partner school. Compare and discuss the advantages and disadvantages of your school systems.

   (ii) Plan an ideal school curriculum and produce a presentation to persuade your head teacher to introduce it in your school.

   (iii) Use one of the ideas from Activity 13 in the skills development activities on page 15, for your project.

> If you are choosing your own project, remember to set a SMART outcome.

Activity 3.1

Think about which research questions or project outcome you would like to try from the box above. You can use the next few activities to help you research, think and decide.

What information do I need?

To answer your research question, you'll need to work out what information you need. For example, for the suggested research question listed in part **(a) (i)** above, you might ask:

- What are the problems in the education system in my country?
- What causes these problems?
- What are the consequences of these problems?

You should also think about the *kind* of information you need. This might be definitions, facts, opinions, value judgments, or predictions (see page 8).

Activity 3.2

(a) What kind of information do you need to answer each of the following questions?

  (i)   What is an IGCSE®?

  (ii) How is education different from knowledge?

  (iii) What proportion of children in your country complete secondary education?

  (iv) What will happen if you don't go to school?

  (v)   Who should fund education?

  (vi) What subjects are compulsory in your school?

  (vii) Why do young people sometimes refuse to go to school?

(b) Work in a group with other people who are interested in the same research question as you. Discuss the following questions, and draw diagrams or use tables to note your ideas.

  (i)   What questions should you ask to help you find information?

  (ii) What kind of information will help you answer each of your questions?

> Remember your class rules about discussions.

Finding information

To find information, you need to:

- use the right search terms (see page 5)
- skim-read long documents, looking for key words (see page 6)
- read small parts of documents for detail (see page 6).

Activity 3.3

(a) What search terms will help you find information and ideas to answer these questions?

  (i)   What proportion of children in your country complete secondary education?

  (ii) What will happen if you don't go to school?

  (iii) Who should fund education?

  (iv) Why do young people sometimes refuse to go to school?

(b) What search terms will help you answer the questions you identified in part (b) (i) of Activity 3.2?

(c) What key words will you look for in documents when you start to search for information?

> Do you need to use the Internet to answer all these questions? How else could you find out this information?

> If you can't find the information you need, change your search terms.

Question

Once you have found a piece of information, always ask yourself the following questions about it:

- Is this a fact, an opinion, a prediction, or a value judgment?
- Do I agree with the opinions given?
- What are the causes and consequences here?
- What are its personal, national and global perspectives?

Activity 3.4

Tishan: "I'd love to study to be a doctor, but my family needs the money I can earn. I'm working in a bank now. It's a good job, but I hate it. It's like living in a box when I dream of the sky. It seems so unfair that some of my friends are at school and hating it, while I can't go."

Colin: "In my opinion, we should change the education system. School should be free, but only for people who work hard and get good results. Then no one would waste time or misbehave, and those of us who want to learn could get on with it."

Ruby: "My parents have made me stay at school to do maths. I'm lucky to have parents who value education, but this is the wrong education for me. All I want to do is work in my uncle's goldsmithing business. I should be able to choose my own future."

(a) Tishan says, "…my family needs the money I can earn." Is this a fact or an opinion? Explain your answer.

(b) Identify one opinion that Tishan gives. Explain your answer.

(c) Identify one value judgment and one prediction that Colin makes.

(d) Identify one opinion and one value judgment in Ruby's words. Explain your answers.

(e) What might be the consequences if everyone or no one had to pay for education?

(f) What might be the consequences if education were free only for people who worked hard and got good results? Think about the national and global perspectives as well as the personal.

(g) What do you think are the causes of bad behaviour in schools?

(h) From a national perspective, is it more important to train people to be economically productive or to be personally fulfilled? Give reasons for your answer.

> Whose view is closest to yours? Why? Discuss this!

Activity 3.5

(a) Make a final choice of research questions for your individual research. Use the skills you have been practising to help you to research ideas, information and perspectives.

(b) Look through your research materials for your individual research.

    (i) Make sure you know when you are reading facts, opinions, predictions, and value judgments.

> Remember to respect other people's opinions even when you don't agree with them.

> **(ii)** Think about which opinions you agree with, and which you don't. Work in a group to discuss the opinions.
>
> **(iii)** Draw diagrams and tables to show the causes and consequences in the issue you've chosen.
>
> **(iv)** Draw diagrams to help you think about the personal, national and global perspectives.
>
> **(v)** Do you need to find any more information? What else do you need to know?

Reflect and plan

Take some time to think about the information, ideas, issues, and perspectives that you have been researching. At this stage you can also start to plan your group project.

Activity 3.6

(a) You should now have thought about education in some new ways. Think about what you have learned and why this might broaden your perspective.

(b) Have you changed your mind about anything? If so, in what way? If not, why not?

Work in groups to discuss questions **(c)** to **(f)**. Afterwards, let the different ideas and opinions float around in your mind for a few days. Keep thinking about them.

(c) In education, which of these do you think is more important, and why?

    (i) Personal fulfilment or a well-paid job? (Does it make a difference if you're young or old?)

    (ii) Academic learning or learning for life?

    (iii) A young person's aims for the future or a parent's aims for their child?

(d) How could we share resources out so that people who want to study can do so?

(e) How should we provide the best opportunities for people who struggle at school?

(f) "Education isn't about fairness. It's about maximizing gain for you, your family, and your country." Do you agree?

Activity 3.7

Work in teams to decide on and plan your project.

(a) Agree on a project outcome.

(b) Decide on team roles, for example who will be the leader.

(c) Copy and complete the table.

Task	Who will do it	When it should be done

Make your table as long as it needs to be for all the tasks.

Present and take action

You have now had time to reflect on the information, ideas, issues, and perspectives for your research report.

Activity 3.8

Write a research report of 300–500 words on your chosen question. Use these headings:

- The problem
- The causes of the problem
- The consequences
- Personal, national, and global perspectives
- The possible solution
  (give your opinions here to answer the question)

Remember

When you write your research report:

▶ use your own words

▶ use clear, simple sentences

▶ give reasons to support your opinions.

Activity 3.9

Carry out your group project. Then answer these questions:

(a) How well did your team work together?

(b) What problems did you have?

(c) How did you solve these problems?

(d) How will you avoid these problems next time?

Section 1
4 Sport and recreation

Figure 4.1 What does sport mean to you?

In this chapter, you are going to work through the Global Perspectives learning process. As described in the skills development activities on pages 1–17, this process involves taking the following steps:

1. Research information

2. Question

3. Reflect and plan

4. Present and take action

You are going to go through this process as you prepare for and complete a short practice individual research report and a mini group project on the topic. You will also be practising and using the skills you started to learn in the skills development activities for this section.

Research information

By following the steps in this chapter, you'll develop the skills that will enable you to produce two good pieces of work: a research report and a group project. First, you will need to choose one research question and one project from the lists in the box above Activity 4.1 and then research relevant information.

Suggested mini research questions and mini project outcomes

(a) Choose one of these research questions.

   (i)   How can we prevent problems of violence at international sporting events (such as football matches)?

   (ii) What are the best solutions to the problems of unfairness in sport?

   (iii) How can we encourage more young women to take up a sport?

   (iv) How can we prevent young people becoming violent in their leisure time?

(b) Choose one of these projects.

   (i)   Make a photo display of different national sports and recreations. Discuss what your national sports and recreations mean to you, and how you think they affect the national character.

   (ii) Design a public information advertisement – in the form of a poster or film – explaining the value of regular exercise and recreation.

   (iii) Use one of the ideas from Activity 13 in the skills development activities on page 15, for your project.

> If you are choosing your own project, remember to set a SMART outcome.

Activity 4.1

Think about which research questions or project outcome you would like to try from the box above. You can use the next few activities to help you research, think and decide.

What information do I need?

To answer your research question, you'll need to work out what information you need. For example, for the suggested research question listed in part **(a) (ii)** above, you might ask:

- What are the problems of unfairness in international sport?
- What causes these problems?
- What are the consequences of these problems?

You should also think about the *kind* of information you need. This might be definitions, facts, opinions, value judgments, or predictions (see page 8).

Activity 4.2

(a) What kind of information do you need to answer each of the following questions?

    (i) What is recreation?

    (ii) How is recreation different from sport?

    (iii) What proportion of women engage in a sport?

    (iv) Will Uruguay win the World Cup?

    (v) Who should fund national sports development programmes?

    (vi) What is the average age at which girls or boys stop doing sport?

    (vii) Why do young people sometimes become violent in their leisure time?

(b) Work in a group with other people who are interested in the same research question as you. Discuss the following questions, and draw diagrams or use tables to note your ideas.

    (i) What questions should you ask to help you find information?

    (ii) What kind of information will help you answer each of your questions?

> Remember your class rules about discussions.

Finding information

To find information, you need to:

- use the right search terms (see page 5)
- skim-read long documents, looking for key words (see page 6)
- read small parts of documents for detail (see page 6).

Activity 4.3

(a) What search terms will help you find information and ideas to answer these questions?

    (i) How is recreation important to individuals and nations?

    (ii) Who should fund national sports development programmes?

    (iii) What is the average age at which girls stop doing sport?

    (iv) Why do young people sometimes become violent in their leisure time?

(b) What search terms will help you answer the questions you identified in part **(b) (i)** of Activity 4.2?

(c) What key words will you look for in documents when you start to search for information?

> Do you need to use the Internet to answer all these questions? How else could you find out this information?

> If you can't find the information you need, change your search terms.

Question

Once you have found a piece of information, always ask yourself the following questions about it:

● Is this a fact, an opinion, a prediction, or a value judgment?

● Do I agree with the opinions given?

● What are the causes and consequences here?

● What are its personal, national and global perspectives?

Activity 4.4

> Keira: "In my opinion, everyone should have to learn and practise a martial art, a form of dance, and cookery. These are really fundamental aspects of human nature. If we introduced this as a policy, there would be far fewer problems with dissatisfied, unhappy people. And therefore we'd have fewer issues with gangs, street violence, and crime. It would also make us more equal."
>
> Hassan: "It's wrong that they make children do sport at school. It's so embarrassing and humiliating for people like me. I just can't do sport. I like walking and cycling, and this keeps me healthy. But why would I want to kick a ball into a net, anyway?"
>
> Bina: "For me, the problem with school sport is that it's all about competition, and being the best. It's supposed to feed into national sport. But only a small proportion of young people become elite athletes in national teams. The rest of us just get bored and give up. Really, though, sport and exercise should be for everyone. We all need to be fit."

(a) Keira says, "These are really fundamental aspects of human nature." Is this a fact or an opinion? Explain your answer.

(b) Identify one prediction that Keira makes. Explain your answer.

(c) Identify one value judgment that Hassan makes. Explain your answer.

(d) Identify one fact and one opinion in Bina's words. Explain your answers.

(e) What might be the consequences if we did not have school sport?

(f) What might be the consequences if schools concentrated on fun exercise instead of competitive sport?

(g) Which is better, in your opinion: competition or exercise just for fun? Give reasons for your answer.

(h) From a national perspective, is it more important to find elite athletes for national teams or to encourage everyone to be fit and healthy? Give reasons for your answer.

Do you agree with Keira? If so, why? If not, why not? Discuss this!

Activity 4.5

(a) Make a final choice of research questions for your individual research. Use the skills you have been practising to help you to research ideas, information and perspectives.

(b) Look through your research materials for your individual research.

    (i) Make sure you know when you are reading facts, opinions, predictions, and value judgments.

    (ii) Think about which opinions you agree with, and which you don't. Work in a group to discuss the opinions.

    (iii) Draw diagrams and tables to show the causes and consequences in the issue you've chosen.

    (iv) Draw diagrams to help you think about the personal, national and global perspectives.

    (v) Do you need to find any more information? What else do you need to know?

> Remember to respect other people's opinions even when you don't agree with them.

Reflect and plan

Take some time to think about the information, ideas, issues, and perspectives that you have been researching. At this stage you can also start to plan your group project.

Activity 4.6

(a) You should now have thought about sport and recreation in some new ways. Think about what you have learned and why this might broaden your perspective.

(b) Have you changed your mind about anything? If so, in what way? If not, why not?

Work in groups to discuss questions **(c)** to **(f)**. Afterwards, let the different ideas and opinions float around in your mind for a few days. Keep thinking about them.

(c) In sport, which of these do you think is more important, and why?

    (i) Health and fitness or competitive success? (Does it make a difference if you're young or old?)

    (ii) Enjoyment or competitive success?

    (iii) National teams or local sporting communities?

(d) How far should parents and coaches push talented young sportspeople? Explain your opinion.

(e) It doesn't matter what hobby you have, as long as you have one. Do you agree? Explain your opinion.

(f) It doesn't matter whether sport is fair; it just needs to be exciting. Do you agree? Explain your opinion.

Activity 4.7

Work in teams to decide on and plan your project.

(a) Agree on a project outcome.

(b) Decide on team roles, for example who will be the leader.

(c) Copy and complete the table.

Task	Who will do it	When it should be done
1		
2		
3		
4		

Make your table as long as it needs to be for all the tasks.

Present and take action

You have now had time to reflect on the information, ideas, issues, and perspectives for your research report.

Activity 4.8

Write a research report of 300–500 words on your chosen question. Use these headings:

- The problem
- The causes of the problem
- The consequences
- Personal, national, and global perspectives
- The possible solution
  (give your opinions here to answer the question)

Remember

When you write your research report:

▶ use your own words

▶ use clear, simple sentences

▶ give reasons to support your opinions.

Activity 4.9

Carry out your group project. Then answer these questions:

(a) How well did your team work together?

(b) What problems did you have?

(c) How did you solve these problems?

(d) How will you avoid these problems next time?

Section 2
Skills development activities

The Global Perspectives learning process – research information, question, reflect and plan, present and take action – is a process that you need to repeat and practise. The activities in this section will help you develop the skills you started to learn in Section 1. Becoming good at this sort of learning is like getting better at a sport or at playing a musical instrument. Successful footballers don't say, "No, I'm not going to practise kicking the ball into the net; we've already done that." Even if you think you have already covered a skill, remember that you are doing it in more depth this time and that practice will make you better at it.

Research information

In this section you'll be working with your teacher to break the big topics down into smaller issues and to think of questions that will help you find the information you need. You will be using the main topic areas covered in this section:

- Biodiversity and ecosystem loss
- Climate change
- Water, food and agriculture
- Fuel and energy.

Concentrate here on the process you are using; in Section 3 you'll be going through this process again but in groups or pairs, with less help from your teacher.

When you are breaking down a big topic, you can use three strategies:

1. Ask all the questions you can think of in a class or group discussion and write down as many ideas as possible.

2. Ask yourself what are the really important, key issues.

3. For each idea or key issue, consider the personal, national and global perspectives.

> **Remember**
>
> Follow the rules you set for class discussions. Listening to other people's ideas is a really good way of sparking new ideas.

Breaking down the topic

The following diagram shows some of the ways you could begin to break down the topic "Water, food and agriculture" by asking various questions. When you do this, remember to think about questions that need different types of answer (see page 4).

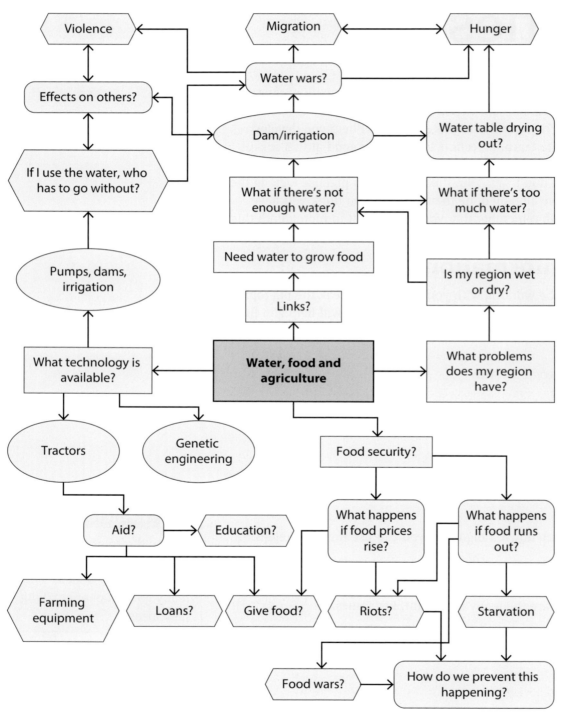

Figure 1 Some first ideas about the topic "Water, food and agriculture". What other ideas do you have?

Activity 1

(a) Identify three questions in Figure 1 that need different kinds of answer – one that needs a fact, one that needs a prediction, and one that needs an opinion or value judgment.

(b) Which of the questions in Figure 1 is most interesting to you? Give your reasons.

(c) What sort of answers to this question do you need – facts, predictions, opinions, or value judgments?

(d) What search terms would you use to find information and ideas to help you answer this question? Think of three or four different ways of searching. See which one produces the most useful results.

(e) What other questions would you like to ask about the topic "Water, food and agriculture"?

(f) In a class discussion on the topic "Fuel and energy", ask plenty of questions to break the topic down into smaller issues.

(g) Working in groups of four or five, discuss either "Biodiversity and ecosystem loss" or "Climate change". Ask plenty of questions in your group to break the topic down into smaller issues.

What is an issue and what is a fact?

An issue is a topic or problem that can be debated or discussed. Issues are usually matters of opinion, value judgment, or prediction. Facts are useful to make sure that the debate is realistic but, on their own, they are not issues. After all, how do you debate or discuss a fact?

For example, let's look at some questions about "Water, food and agriculture".

● "Is my region wet or dry?" This question does not raise an issue – it's not a problem for discussion or debate. How wet or dry your region is can be established by looking at weather records.

● "What will happen if drought or flooding means there is not enough food in my region?" This question does raise an issue. It's a real problem that needs to be discussed so that solutions can be found.

● "How can we avoid water wars in dry regions?" This question does raise an issue. It's a real problem that can't be answered with facts. There isn't an easy answer, so there is a need for discussion and debate to find a solution.

Activity 2

(a) Which of these questions raise issues?

  (i) What do we need fuel/energy for?

  (ii) If we stopped using oil, what would be the cost to the economy?

  (iii) Why does it matter if the coral reefs die?

  (iv) Is genetic engineering the best way to ensure food security?

  (v) Is hydro-electricity efficient?

  (vi) Is it reasonable for developing nations to keep using oil to boost their economies, even though this contributes to global warming?

  (vii) Could we use some of the plants in the rainforest for medicines?

(b) Look back at the questions you thought of in Activity 1, part (e). Which of these questions raise issues?

(c) Look back at the questions you thought of in Activity 1, part (f). Which of these questions raise issues?

Moving from facts to issues

There may be times when the questions you can think of are factual, and not about issues. If you ask further questions, you can move from the facts to the issues:

● Why do I need to know this information?

● What consequences could come from this fact?

The following diagram shows that from the fact "My region is wet" arises the issue "How do we cope with homelessness due to flooding?"

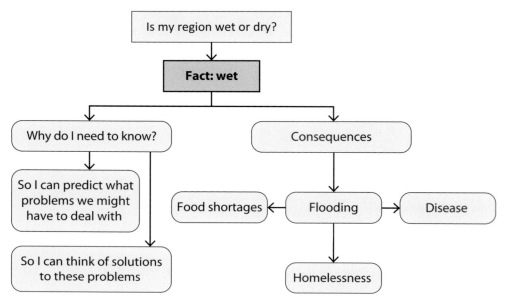

Figure 2 Identifying issues from a fact: ask why you need to know and what might be the possible consequences

---

Activity 3

For each of the following facts, ask why you need to know and what the consequences could be. Draw diagrams if it helps you. What issues do these questions lead you to?

(a) We need fuel for factories, computers, travelling, lighting, and keeping our homes warm.

(b) Hydro-electricity is very efficient.

(c) Birds and bats eat mosquitoes.

(d) The rainforest is the source of many plants that are used to make medicines.

Identifying key issues

Key issues are the really important problems that need to be discussed.
Some of the things that determine the importance of a problem include:

- consequences
- urgency
- severity
- perspectives.

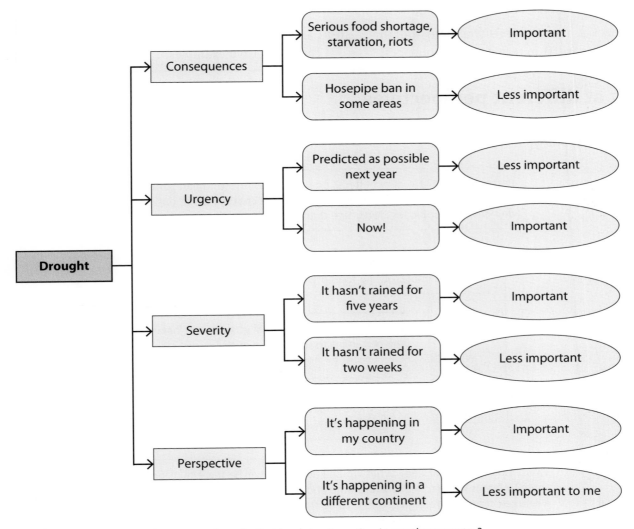

Figure 3 How important is a severe drought that leads to starvation in another country?

Activity 4

(a) Think about some of the issues in Figure 1 in terms of consequences, urgency, severity, and perspectives. Draw diagrams if it helps you. Which issues are the most important? Why?

(b) Look back at the questions you thought of in Activity 1, part (e) in terms of consequences, urgency, severity, and perspectives. Draw diagrams if it helps you. Which are most important? Why?

(c) Look back at the questions you thought of in Activity 1, part (f) in terms of consequences,

urgency, severity, and perspectives. Draw diagrams if it helps you. Which are the most important? Why?

(d) How does where you live influence your answers? For example, if you live in a dry country, are you more worried about problems related to drought than too much water?

(e) Can you see how different national perspectives can arise? Give examples.

Looking at different perspectives

Looking at personal, national and global perspectives can help you organize your ideas and your research.

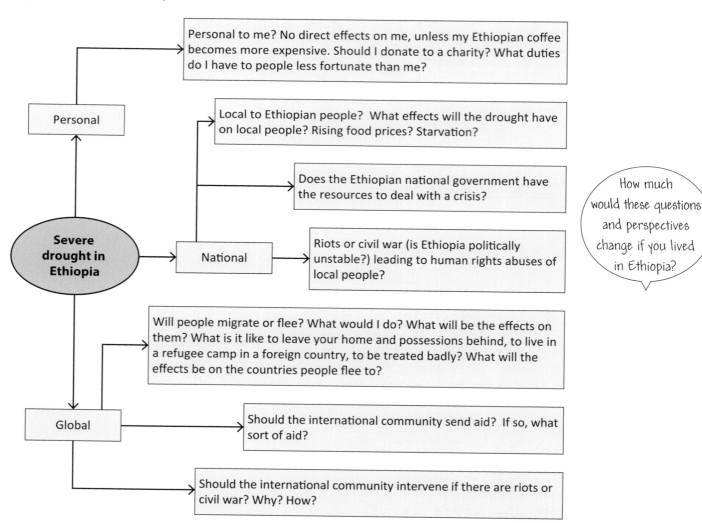

Figure 4 Different perspectives on a local drought. Can you think of any others?

Sometimes perspectives aren't clearly personal, national or global, but a mixture. For example:

● your own personal perspective might just be, "Should I donate to a charity to help people who are starving?" but this question is also important globally: should my country give aid?

● the perspective of the people who are leaving their homes and who become refugees also links to the global perspective of how to deal with refugees.

Make sure you consider all three perspectives – personal, national, and global – for each key issue, using Internet searches and diagrams.

> Think about the search terms you use. For example, "Global Perspective Drought" might not be enough.

Activity 5

(a) Do the following comments express personal, national or global perspectives? Do some of them have mixed perspectives?

(i) "We have plenty of oil in our country, and we need to use it to develop our economy. Why should we use less because people in developed countries, which are already rich, are worried about climate change? Poverty will kill our people faster than global warming."

(ii) "Even a small rise in sea level will flood us in the Maldives, because 80 per cent of our islands are less than a metre above sea level. People in the West have got to stop burning oil to make their lives more convenient – it's destroying my home."

(iii) "The Maldives are going to be flooded? Well, I'll just have to take my holidays on a Caribbean island instead."

(iv) "The UN has to work with national governments to reduce ecosystem destruction around the world. These ecosystems provide global benefits – for example, the rainforest provides oxygen for us all to breathe – and they also provide local benefits. Natural ecosystems such as forests, wetlands, and coastal systems can provide barriers that prevent natural disasters from harming as many people. They also provide water, wood, food, and medicines, which can help communities recover from natural disasters."

(b) Ethiopia wants to build a dam on the Nile near the border with Sudan and upstream of Egypt. What are the different perspectives on this? Use Internet searches and diagrams to help you.

(c) Half of Australia's Great Barrier Reef, the world's largest coral reef ecosystem, disappeared between 1985 and 2012. What are the different personal, local/national and global perspectives on this? Use Internet searches and diagrams to help you.

(d) Oil is getting harder to find and extract. This means that prices are rising. What are the different personal, local/national and global perspectives on this? Use Internet searches and diagrams to help you.

(e) Look back at the questions and key issues you thought of in Activity 1, part **(e)**. What are the different personal, local/national and global perspectives? Use Internet searches and diagrams to help you.

(f) Look back at the questions and key issues you thought of in Activity 1, part **(f)**. What are the different personal, local/national and global perspectives? Use Internet searches and diagrams to help you.

Finding the gaps in your knowledge

So far we've been thinking about how you can find information and ideas on a big topic about which you know little or nothing. Even if you research plenty of information, there may still be small gaps in your knowledge that need to be filled in. Identifying what you need to know to fill these small gaps is also an important skill. Let's look at an example.

> Nuclear power stations do not produce as many carbon emissions as coal-fired power stations. This means they are better for the environment, so the government should invest in nuclear power stations.

This seems to make sense. But there are gaps in our knowledge. In order to decide whether the government should invest in nuclear power stations, we need to know about:

- the carbon emissions involved in constructing the different power stations
- the carbon emissions involved in mining, extracting, and transporting the raw materials (coal and uranium)
- the carbon emissions involved in decommissioning nuclear power plants
- the length of time a nuclear power plant will last
- other environmental problems, such as the problems with radioactive nuclear waste, possible health effects on local populations, and the possibility of another disaster like Chernobyl or Fukushima
- the total carbon emissions from energy sources such as wind, sun, and tide.

This is a skill that may by tested in the written examination. You should also use this skill in your research and project planning. For example, if you are planning a dinner, and you've sent 16 invitations, you need to know how many people have accepted the invitation. This will help you buy the right amount of food.

Activity 6

Read the following comments. What else do you need to know?

(a) "Genetic engineering (GE) can make plants resistant to pests, cold, and drought. These GE crops can save us from food shortages. The green movement should therefore stop its opposition to GE crops."

(b) "John and Jasvinder are setting up a company to manufacture environmentally friendly products. We should invest in their company."

Making notes

When you are researching information and ideas on the Internet, it is a good idea to make brief notes, and keep a list of which source these ideas came from. You will need to look at a lot of material. Work smarter, not harder!

Do:

✓ skim-read when looking for relevant and important ideas

✓ identify short passages to read carefully

✓ write key words or phrases

✓ use diagrams to show causes, consequences, perspectives, etc.

✓ write your own questions – about things you don't understand, about things you need to know, about differences of opinion…

✓ use different colours – if your own questions are in different colours, you'll be able to find them, and if causes and consequences are in different colours, you might be able to spot a pattern

✓ copy one or two significant sentences that you might want to quote

✓ record the website URL in your notes, with the date

✓ write down the title and author of a book, with the page number(s) by each idea.

Don't:

✗ read everything on every website you find

✗ write down everything

✗ copy and paste everything

✗ use other people's words without quoting and referencing.

Activity 7

The Australian Great Barrier Reef is disappearing. Research the causes and consequences of this.

(a) Think about your search terms.

(b) Make structured notes of no more than 100 words. You may use diagrams.

(c) Make a note of which ideas are related to which sources and keep a list of sources.

Providing references

When you present your work, it is important to provide references for ideas you have taken from your sources. So remember to make a note of them while you are researching! There are a number of styles of reference (or citation). You can use any, but be consistent. The following table shows what to include for different sources, with an example for each.

Source	What to include	Example
Website	<ul><li>URL</li><li>Date you accessed the website</li><li>Author, if there is one</li></ul>	http://www.livescience.com/23612-great-barrier-reef-steep-decline.html, accessed 04.04.14, written by Katherine Gammon
Book	<ul><li>Author(s)</li><li>Title</li><li>Publisher</li><li>Date of publication</li><li>Page number(s)</li></ul>	A. Imeson, *Desertification, Land Degradation and Sustainability* (Wiley, 2011), p. 211
Journal article	<ul><li>Author(s)</li><li>Title of paper</li><li>Title and volume of journal</li><li>Page number(s)</li></ul>	L.E. Venegas; N.A Mazzeo, "Traffic Pollution Modelling in a Complex Urban Street", *International Journal of Environment and Pollution*, Vol 48/2, pp. 87–95

Question

In Section 1 you questioned the ideas and information you found, mostly by identifying facts, opinions, predictions, value judgments, causes, and consequences. In this section you are going to start to question ideas and information in a more evaluative way – that is, by deciding how valuable they are.

Evaluating sources

When you find information and ideas in a source – a website, a book, a newspaper, or a journal – you can question what you find by asking:

- How reliable is the source?
- How good is the reasoning?
- How likely are the causes and consequences they suggest?

> Go to the "About us" page of a website for information that may help you decide whether the source is reliable.

How reliable is the source?

You can ask questions about the source of information, and check up on the source to find out if it's reliable.

- How serious is this newspaper/journal/website, or how sensationalist? Is it a social media site?
- Could this be true – in other words, is it plausible – or is it too unlikely or unrealistic – implausible?
- Is the author an expert? Has the author researched properly or is he or she a teenager just writing opinions on a social media site?
- Does the author have a reason to lie or only tell part of the truth?

- Does the author have a reputation for being untruthful? If so, how much does this matter?

- Are there opinions pretending to be facts?

Watch out for fakes and hoaxes, misunderstandings, and mistakes.

For example, this is taken from Richard Branson's blog on 1 April 2013:

'I'm thrilled to announce that Virgin has created another world-first with the introduction of the technology required to produce the world's first glass-bottomed plane.'

Source: http://www.virgin.com/richard-branson/virgin-atlantic-launches-worlds-first-ever-glass-bottomed-plane

This seems like a genuine news story from a reliable businessman. However, it was in fact an April Fool's joke – a hoax.

Activity 8

(a) Look at this website. It includes information on a number of Internet hoaxes,

http://urbanlegends.about.com/od/reference/a/top_25_uls.htm

(b) Do you think this extract is telling the truth, or is it a hoax?

"NASA is planning a $2.6 billion robotic mission to catch an asteroid in a giant bag and tow it to the Moon as part of a long-term programme that could one day lead to the permanent settlement of humans in space."

Source: http://www.thetimes.co.uk/tto/science/space/article3727898.ece

(c) For situations (i) and (ii), who would be a reliable source of information?

(i) A disagreement between two of your friends, Sala and Preetha. Who would be a reliable source of information? Think about ways in which each one might not be reliable – why not?

- Preetha's best friend who did not see what happened

- A teacher who dislikes Sala and saw the incident

- Ramesh, who saw what happened, and who has sometimes been known to tell tales to get attention. He is not particularly good friends with either Sala or Preetha.

(ii) There has been an oil leak from a deep sea oil pipe which is affecting the coastal ecosystems across three countries. You want to find out what really happened. Which of the following would be a reliable source? What makes you think that?

- The oil company's representative

- Divers who recently serviced the oil pipe

- The government of the country that owns the oil pipe

- A sensationalist newspaper in a country affected by the oil leak

- A professor at an elite university. She has studied the causes of oil leaks around the world.

(d) Go back to one of your Internet searches earlier in this section. Look at your sources and ask yourself whether they are reliable. Think about the type of source (serious journal, social media site), whether what it says is likely to be true, and whether the author is an expert or has a reason to lie or a reputation for lying.

How good is the reasoning in the sources?

When an author is expressing an opinion, or persuading the audience to accept a proposal, you can also ask how well their reasoning works. Think about the questions shown in this table.

Questions to ask about reasoning	Yes/No
1 Has the author given reasons for their opinion or proposal?	
2 Do the reasons support the opinion logically in general?	
3 Are the reasons based on strong evidence?	
4 Has the author used emotion instead of reason to make you agree?	
5 Are there gaps between the reasons and the proposal or opinion?	

Your answers to 1, 2, and 3 should be yes and your answers to 4 and 5 should be no.

Let's look at the following examples.

> "The Ethiopians want to build a dam on the Nile. They're stealing our water. We should explode the ships bringing materials for the dam so they can't build it."

Comment: "They're stealing our water" is using emotion to persuade us – after all, what makes it "our" water? This is also not a strong enough reason to explode ships. Perhaps negotiation would be a better alternative? We need to know many more facts about the planned dam, about agreements between the countries regarding the water, and about the likely consequences of exploding their ships, so this reasoning doesn't work well.

> "We're running out of oil. If we keep using oil like this, there will be no oil left by 2025. So the government should ban us from using cars."

Comment: The claim about running out of oil is not based on strong evidence; it would need to be supported – and might be unlikely. There are also gaps between the reasons why we are running out of oil and the proposal that the government should ban us from using cars. We need to know why this is the right action to take. The reasoning doesn't work well here, so this is a weak and illogical argument.

Activity 9

In these opinions from Activity 5, how well does the reasoning work? You have already thought about the personal, national and global perspectives. Concentrate now on whether they are logical.

(a) "We have plenty of oil in our country, and we need to use it to develop our economy. Why should we use less because people in developed countries, which are already rich, are worried about climate change? Poverty will kill our people faster than global warming."

(b) "Even a small rise in sea level will flood us in the Maldives, because 80 per cent of our islands are less than a metre above sea level. People in the West have got to stop burning oil to make their lives more convenient – it's destroying my home."

(c) "The Maldives are going to be flooded? Well, I'll just have to take my holidays on a Caribbean island instead."

(d) "The UN has to work with national governments to reduce ecosystem destruction around the world. These ecosystem provide global benefits – for example, the rainforest provides oxygen for us all to breathe – and they also provide local benefits. Natural ecosystems such as forests, wetlands, and coastal systems can provide barriers that prevent natural disasters from harming as many people. They also provide water, wood, food, and medicines, which can help communities recover from natural disasters."

Evaluating causes and consequences

Two of the most important ways of evaluating reasoning about causes and consequences are:

- considering possible alternative causes and consequences
- considering how likely a consequence is.

Considering possible alternatives

Whenever a cause or consequence is suggested, think about whether there might be alternatives. For example:

> "Delilah arrives home from school sopping wet. Her mother says, 'Oh, is it raining?'"

Here, Delilah's mother is looking for a cause for her daughter's wetness. Rain seems to be a likely cause (at least, if you live in a fairly rainy climate) – but there are alternatives. Perhaps some other students threw water at Delilah, or perhaps she lay in the river with all her clothes on to cool off. Even if these other possible causes of Delilah's wetness seem unlikely, they are worth considering – especially if you look outside and discover that it is not raining.

Let's look at another example.

> "If we invest in nuclear power stations, we will significantly reduce our carbon emissions."

Here, the predicted consequence is that we will reduce our carbon emissions, but other consequences are possible. For example, we might actually produce *more* carbon emissions because we are using more power, in the belief that it is "clean", and we might also produce significant quantities of radioactive waste.

Activity 10

(a) Suggest alternative causes for the following statements:

    (i) "The main cause of disagreements about water use in the Nile basin is the growing population."

    (ii) "The main cause of destruction of natural ecosystems is greed."

(b) Suggest alternative consequences for the following statements:

    (i) "There are two new sources of fossil fuel – 'fracking' and methane hydrate. As a consequence, we do not need to worry about fuel running out."

    (ii) "If we build an offshore wind farm, the local residents will enjoy a cheap source of clean fuel."

(c) Go back to one of the issues you considered in Activity 4. Review the consequences you predicted. Can you think of any alternatives?

How likely is it?

When you are considering causes and consequences, you need to think about how likely a consequence is. To do this, you need to take lots of circumstances into consideration.

Let's look at a situation from school life.

Cause	Possible consequences	Likely?
Adam hits the teacher.	The teacher respects Adam and stops giving him homework.	Highly unlikely in any well-run school.
	The teacher hits Adam back.	Unlikely in countries where teachers are forbidden from hitting students.
		More likely where there are no such laws.
		Could depend on whether anyone is looking. Could also depend on who is bigger and stronger.
	Adam is told off but is given no punishment.	This is quite unlikely because it doesn't reflect the seriousness of what Adam has done.
	Adam is sent on an anger management course	This is quite likely in a British school, especially if Adam often has problems controlling his temper. In other countries it might be less likely.
	Adam is given a serious punishment but allowed to remain in the school.	This is likely in many schools. It might depend on what Adam's behaviour is normally like.
	Adam is expelled from school.	This is likely in a strict school. In other schools it would be less likely if it were the first time Adam had misbehaved. It might depend on why Adam hit the teacher.

Activity 11

(a) For each of the following events, think of all the possible consequences you can, and then decide which are the most likely, and why.

    (i) We fly to the Maldives on holiday.

    (ii) We invest in methane hydrate.

    (iii) We drill down to the water table to get water to irrigate our crops.

    (iv) We invest in ways of harvesting more rainwater.

(b) Play this game in teams:

- One member of Team A describes an event.

- Team B has to think of a consequence.

Award two points if Team C/the teacher thinks it is very likely, one point for likely, zero points for unlikely. Award one bonus point for being amusing.

Reflect and plan

Now is the time to think quietly about all the research and the questioning and evaluation you have done so far in this section.

Activity 12

(a) Have you formed new opinions or changed your mind about any of the issues described in this section? Give your reasons why or why not.

(b) Have you needed to question your value judgments?

(c) How does your personal perspective link to national and global perspectives on each issue?

(d) What did you think of this comment (from Activity 5)? "The Maldives are going to be flooded? Well, I'll have to take my holidays on a Caribbean island instead." Why did you think this?

(e) Have you needed to question your actions? Will you make any changes to the way you use resources and fuel?

(f) What links are there between the four topics in this section? Use a spider diagram like the ones in this section to show the links.

(g) What do you think is the most important issue covered in this section? Why is it so important? Why is it most important to you?

(h) Write three questions for each topic to help you think more deeply about your opinions, value judgments, and actions.

Spend time thinking about these questions. Keep coming back to them. Reflection is not a task you can do and then tick the box; it's an ongoing process.

Project planning

As a practice run before you plan and carry out your assessed group project, you are going to plan and carry out a small, simple project in teams. It will have an active outcome.

In Section 1 we looked at SMART outcomes for an active project. You need to think about these every time you plan a project.

Activity 13

(a) Look at the following ideas for projects organized by a group of 14–16-year-olds. Are they SMART outcomes?

   (i)   Prevent conflict over water in the Nile basin.

   (ii) Write a letter to the Egyptian and Ethiopian ambassadors in your country, asking them to persuade their governments to co-operate over the use of Nile waters.

   (iii) Stop/reduce oil and water usage for a month, note the personal consequences, and present your group's findings to the school.

   (iv) Design and produce tee-shirts or mugs to show key issues in a topic you have studied.

   (v) Design and produce a water-saving device and present its advantages to your community.

(b) What actions would you like to take in each of these topic areas? Are your actions SMART?

   (i)   Biodiversity and ecosystem loss

   (ii) Climate change

   (iii) Water, food and agriculture

   (iv) Fuel and energy

Making your mini project plan

For your group mini project, you are going to organize a tea party or coffee morning with a theme, to raise money for a charity. Use the following prompts and the table below to help you.

- Which charity? Why
- Which theme? Why?
- What sort of food and drink will you serve?
- How will you make sure you raise money?
- How will you decide how many and whom to invite?
- Who will send the invitations?
- What else?
- Roles for team members?
- Are we being SMART (Specific, Measurable, Achievable, Realistic, Time-bound)?

> Be careful - are you spending too much time deciding on the theme and forgetting the tasks?

Outcome: themed tea party or coffee morning to raise money for a charity			
Task	**Who**	**When**	**Comments**
Decide theme	Group	Week 1	Habitat loss of wild pandas? Climate change too boring!
Decide menu	Group	Week 2	Could we make panda cakes? Can people even eat bamboo? Does the food even need to reflect the theme?
Send invitations			Before deciding who to invite?

Present and take action

Now that you have researched information, questioned and evaluated it, reflected on it and made a plan, the final stage is to write a presentation of your findings and suggest a course of action.

Writing in clear English

It's important to write in your own words. Practise turning complex language into simpler sentences that make sense to you. For example, you might find a sentence like this:

> "If methane hydrate allows much of the world to switch from oil to gas, the conversion would undermine governments that depend on oil revenues, especially petro-autocracies like Russia, Iran, Venezuela, Iraq, Kuwait, and Saudi Arabia."

Source: http://www.theatlantic.com/magazine/archive/2013/05/what-if-we-never-run-out-of-oil/309294/

Using this source, you could write:

"This fuel could cause problems for governments in oil-rich countries like Iran."

Developing a line of reasoning

When you present your research results, your presentation must have a purpose, as discussed in Section 1. This purpose is likely to be answering a question or supporting a proposal for action. To do this, you need to use reasoning. Reasoning is logical, connected writing. There are two main kinds of reasoning: argument and explanation.

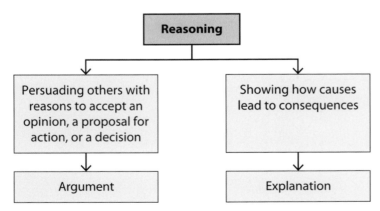

Figure 5 Types of reasoning

An explanation shows how a cause or causes leads to a consequence. For example:

> "There are several causes of the coral reef's decline. The biggest factors are smashing from tropical cyclones, crown-of-thorns starfish that eat coral and are boosted by nutrient runoff from agriculture, and coral bleaching from high temperatures, which are rising due to climate change."

Source: http://www.livescience.com/23612-great-barrier-reef-steep-decline.html

---

Activity 14

Write a simple sentence that summarizes each of these three passages:

(a) "On a broader level still, cheap, plentiful natural gas throws a wrench into efforts to combat climate change. Avoiding the worst effects of climate change, scientists increasingly believe, will require 'a complete phase-out of carbon emissions… over 50 years'."

(b) "'Water scarcity is an issue exacerbated by demographic pressures, climate change and pollution,' said Ignacio Saiz, director of Centre for Economic and Social Rights, a social justice group. 'The world's water supplies should guarantee every member of the population to cover their personal and domestic needs.'"

Source: http://www.aljazeera.com/indepth/features/2011/06/2011622193147231653.html

(c) "Recent scholars, including Thomas Homer-Dixon, have analysed various case studies on environmental degradation to conclude that there is not a direct link between scarcity and violence. Instead, he believes inequality, social inclusion and other factors determine the nature and ferocity of strife."

Source: http://www.aljazeera.com/indepth/features/2011/06/2011622193147231653.html

This explanation shows how coral reef decline has several causes.

An argument uses reasons to persuade us to accept an opinion or proposal. For example:

> "Climate change is threatening the earth in many ways. We have a duty to protect it for future generations. Individually we cannot make big changes, but if each individual contributes, then together we can succeed. So we should work together as a community to reduce our consumption and recycle our waste."

This argument gives reasons why "we should work together as a community to reduce our consumption and recycle our waste". This opinion is the **conclusion** of the argument. It is the main idea that the author wants you to accept.

Reasons and conclusions

When you are presenting your ideas, you normally want to persuade someone to accept your opinion, value judgment, or proposal for action. So you use reasons, and the opinion, value judgment or proposal for action becomes your conclusion.

For example, let's turn an opinion into an argument supporting a conclusion. This diagram shows how to develop an argument from the opinion: "People who don't recycle should have to pay a fine."

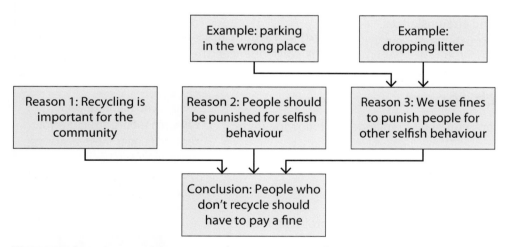

Figure 6a An argument giving reasons that support a conclusion

Mini arguments and mini conclusions

In the argument shown in the diagram you can see that Reason 1 is also an opinion, and Reason 2 is a value judgment. This is okay, but it would make your argument better if you give reasons to support them. If you do this, it will turn your original reasons into mini conclusions. Let's look at supporting Reason 1 as an example: "Recycling is important for the community".

Figure 6b Using reasons to support a mini conclusion

(a) How would you support the value judgment that "People should be punished for selfish behaviour"?

   (i) Can you think of specific circumstances when you would punish people for selfish behaviour?

   (ii) Can you think of specific circumstances when you would not punish people for selfish behaviour?

(b) "Our school community needs to reduce consumption (of goods, energy, water, food…). How can this be done?" Write an argument to persuade the school management to accept one proposal for reducing school consumption. Think about giving reasons. Do you need to support your reasons and turn them into mini conclusions?

(c) Explain what causes climate change and what its consequences are. Use diagrams.

Presenting a research report

When you present a research report, you need to include the following items.

1. Your question
2. Key issues/problems that need to be solved
3. Different perspectives on the key issues
4. An explanation of the causes of the current situation or problem
5. A prediction of the possible consequences of the current situation or problem
6. An evaluation of these consequences: whether they are good or bad, likely or unlikely
7. A suggestion of possible solutions or courses of action

Use these items as headings in your research report. You could also include:

- an explanation of how one course of action could help
- an argument to persuade us to adopt this course of action.

Your work should be your own, and written in simple, clear English. You may use quotations, but not many, and you must reference these.

> To help you organize your research report, structure your research under these headings: Key issues, Perspectives, Causes and consequences, and Possible solutions.

> **Remember**
>
> Make sure you answer your question! You can often do this with your suggested course of action.

> You may already have diagrams that you can use or adapt. Make sure you use the work you have already done.

Section 2
5 Biodiversity and ecosystem loss

Figure 5.1 How can we reduce habitat destruction?

Remember

The Global Perspectives learning process:

▶ Research information

▶ Question

▶ Reflect and plan

▶ Present your findings and take action

In this chapter, you are going to work through the Global Perspectives learning process, as you did in Section 1. As you go through the process, you will practise and develop the skills you have been working on in the skills development activities for this section. You will also apply these skills as you prepare and produce a short research report and a mini project.

Research information

First you will need to think about and choose a research question and a project outcome from the suggestions in the box below.

What is biodiversity? What are ecosystems? Why does it matter if we lose them? How many different kinds of ecosystem can you think of or find out about?

Remember

The skills you'll learn in this section build on and develop the skills you learned in Section 1, so don't forget to use those basic skills as well.

Suggested research questions and project outcomes

(a) Choose one of these research questions.

(i) How can we protect vulnerable ecosystems?

(ii) How can we deal with the problems of decreasing biodiversity?

(iii) A research question agreed with your teacher.

(b) Choose one of these projects.

(i) Make a photo display of different problems associated with ecosystem loss and biodiversity. Explain the causes and consequences of these problems (using diagrams or a short talk).

(ii) Design a set of cartoons that illustrate the personal, national and global problems associated with biodiversity and ecosystem loss. Use these cartoons in a display, or to make mugs or tee-shirts to sell at a school event.

(iii) Use one of the ideas from Activity 13 in the Section 2 skills development activities (page 58) for your project.

> If you are agreeing a research question with your teacher, make sure that the question allows you to look at causes, consequences, personal, national and global perspectives, and possible solutions.

> If you are choosing your own project, remember to set a SMART outcome (see page 14).

Activity 5.1

Think about which research questions or project outcome you would like to try from the list of suggestions. You can use the next few activities to help you research, think and decide.

Breaking down the topic

When you break down a topic, you need to:

● ask plenty of questions and draw diagrams to show the links between them

● consider the key issues

● consider the personal, national and global perspectives.

You've already done some work on breaking down a big topic in the skills development activities in this section, on pages 43–62. Now you can apply this skill to the research question you have chosen, and break it down further into smaller questions you need to answer.

Activity 5.2

What are the personal, national and global consequences, issues, and perspectives that arise from the following?

(a) Why do we need to keep mangroves around Mumbai? Surely there is a cleaner, more modern solution?

(b) In the past 30 years, 297 million farmland birds have been wiped out of existence across Europe.

(c) All the different species on earth depend on one another.

(d) In 2009 alone, 3,000 listed companies around the world were responsible for over $2 trillion in environmental and social costs that have to be borne by society.

(e) Inland wetlands cover at least 9.5 million km² (i.e. about 6.5 per cent of the earth's land surface).

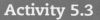

Activity 5.3

(a) To break down your research question, ask more questions, working in a group with other people who have chosen the same research question as you. Use diagrams to help you.

(b) Which of the questions you have asked are key issues? Which of them relate to information that will help you answer?

(c) What personal, national and global perspectives can you think of?

Finding information and ideas

When you are researching information and ideas, you need to think about:

● precise search terms (see page 5)

● gaps in your knowledge (see page 50).

Activity 5.4

(a) Look at each of the small questions you identified in part (a) of Activity 5.3.

    (i)   What search terms do you need?

    (ii) Try several combinations of search terms.

(b) Look over your notes several times while you are researching and ask:

    (i)   Am I finding the right balance of facts, opinions, predictions, and value judgments? If not, how can I change my search terms?

    (ii) How do the information and ideas I am finding help me answer my question?

    (iii) Are there gaps in my knowledge? If so, how can I fill them?

Question

When you are questioning the ideas, information, and perspectives that you have found during your research, you can ask:

● How reliable is the source?

● How good is the reasoning?

● How likely are the causes and consequences?

● Are there alternative possible causes and consequences?

See pages 52–57.

> **Remember**
>
> Other people have personal and national perspectives too.

> Make notes. Organize your notes, and keep them where you can find them.

> If you have too many questions relating to facts, you can move to issues by asking: "Why do I need to know this? What consequences could come from this fact?" If you have too many questions relating to issues, you can ask: "What do I need to know to help me debate these issues?"

> **Remember**
>
> To decide whether an issue is important, you can consider consequences, urgency, severity, and perspectives.

> Make brief, structured notes on any ideas and information you find. Keep a list of the websites you have used.

> **Remember**
>
> Skim-read documents for the gist before reading the relevant parts in more detail.

> Make a note of which search terms are most effective for different kinds of question. Use this to make your searching skills better next time.

Activity 5.5

Adam: "Politicians never think their decisions through or consider the consequences. My uncle was telling me about how they used DDT on mosquitoes to stop malaria, but it just killed all the birds – and we've still got malaria anyway. And they use pesticides that kill bees, so now there are no bees to pollinate our food crops. This is going to be a total disaster – 30 per cent of our food needs to be pollinated. There are already enough hungry people."

Dinesh: "Some people say we should make a set of rules about how our biodiversity – 'genetic resources' – can be used. This is a terrible idea. It will result in a price tag on biodiversity. Another consequence is that we'll only conserve the things we understand the value of. It will be a way of rich countries gaining commercial benefit while poor countries are exploited. Again."

(a) What do you need to know about Adam's uncle to know whether he is a reliable source of information?

(b) How reliable do you think Adam and Dinesh are as sources of information? What do you need to know about them?

(c) How reasonable are the causes and consequences suggested by Adam? Can you spot any exaggeration?

(d) How reasonable are the consequences suggested by Dinesh? Can you think of any plausible alternatives?

(e) What good reasons and evidence does each speaker give to support his views?

(f) Can you spot whether Adam and Dinesh use emotion instead of reasons? Where?

(g) Can you spot opinions pretending to be facts?

Activity 5.6

Look at the sources you have found so far.

(a) How reliable are they? If not very, what will you do?

(b) How good is the reasoning? How will this affect the way you use the ideas, information, and perspectives in your work?

(c) How likely are the causes and consequences? If not very, what will you do?

(d) Are there alternative possible consequences? If so, how will this affect the way you use these ideas in your work?

> If your source is unreliable, look for a more reliable source.

> If the reasoning is poor or the consequences are unlikely, look for better-quality sources of ideas, information, and perspectives. Don't quote material that you have identified as illogical or of poor quality.

Reflect and plan

Activity 5.7

You should now have thought about biodiversity and ecosystem loss in some new ways.

(a) Have you thought about biodiversity and ecosystems in any new ways? If so, what and why?

(b) Have you changed your mind about anything? If so, in what way? If not, why not?

(c) Do you think that animals are as important as humans? If so, in what way? If not, why not?

(d) Are there any ecosystems – such as coastal systems, forests, or mountains – that are important in your life? Why are they important and what value do they have for you?

(e) What is the most important issue you have considered while preparing your research report?

(f) Think of other questions to help you reflect on the issues and perspectives. Let these questions and possible answers to them float around in your mind.

(g) How does your personal perspective link with different national and global perspectives?

(h) Is your personal perspective well thought through? What evidence and reasons can you give to support your perspective?

Activity 5.8

Work in teams to plan your project.

(a) Decide on team roles, for example who will be the leader.

(b) Copy and complete the table.

Task	Who will do it	When it should be done

Make your table as long as it needs to be for all the tasks.

Present and take action

You have now had time to reflect on the information, ideas, issues, and perspectives for your research report.

Activity 5.9

Write a research report of 500–600 words on your chosen question. Use these headings:

- The problem
- The causes of the problem
- The consequences
- Personal, national and global perspectives
- The possible solution
  (give your opinions here to answer the question)

Remember

When you write your research report:

► use your own words

► use clear, simple sentences

► give reasons to support your opinions.

Activity 5.10

Carry out your group project. Then answer these questions:

(a) What was it like working with people from another country/culture?

(b) How well did your team work together?

(c) What problems did you have?

(d) How did you solve these problems?

(e) How will you avoid these problems next time?

Section 2
6 Climate change

Figure 6.1 How can we reduce the impact of climate change?

Remember

The Global Perspectives learning process:

▶ Research information

▶ Question

▶ Reflect and plan

▶ Present your findings and take action

In this chapter, you are going to work through the Global Perspectives learning process, as you did in Section 1. As you go through the process, you will practise and develop the skills you have been working on in the skills development activities for this section. You will also apply these skills as you prepare and produce a short research report and a mini project.

What is climate change? Why does it happen? Why does it affect our planet?

Research information

First you will need to think about and choose a research question and a project outcome from the suggestions in the box below.

Remember

The skills you'll learn in this section build on and develop the skills you learned in Section 1, so don't forget to use those basic skills as well.

Suggested research questions and project outcomes

(a) Choose one of these research questions.

(i) What can individuals and governments do to reduce the impact of climate change on countries like the Maldives?

(ii) How reliable is it for nations to keep using oil, even though this contributes to climate change?

(iii) How can rich countries help less economically developed countries to develop in a cleaner way?

(iv) A research question agreed with your teacher.

(b) Choose one of these projects.

    (i) Make a photo display of different problems associated with climate change. Explain the causes and consequences of these problems (using diagrams or a short talk).

    (ii) Design a set of cartoons that illustrate the personal, national and global problems associated with climate change. Use these cartoons in a display, or to make mugs or tee-shirts to sell at a school event.

    (iii) Use one of the ideas from Activity 13 in the Section 2 skills development activities (page 58) for your project.

> If you are agreeing a research question with your teacher, make sure that the question allows you to look at causes, consequences, personal, national and global perspectives, and possible solutions.

> If you are choosing your own project, remember to set a SMART outcome (see page 14).

Activity 6.1

Think about which research questions or project outcome you would like to try from the list of suggestions. You can use the next few activities to help you research, think and decide.

Breaking down the topic

When you break down a topic, you need to:

- ask plenty of questions and draw diagrams to show the links between them
- consider the key issues
- consider the personal, national and global perspectives.

You've already done some work on breaking down a big topic in the skills development activities in this section, on pages 43–62. Now you can apply this skill to the research question you have chosen, and break it down further into smaller questions you need to answer.

Activity 6.2

What are the personal, national and global consequences, issues, and perspectives that arise from the following?

(a) We're having a really cold summer. We could do with a bit of global warming.

(b) My country is getting hotter and drier, mostly because of pollution made in other countries.

(c) Rapid climate change means that ecosystems can't adapt naturally.

(d) It doesn't matter if environmentally friendly living affects the economy now. Having a future is more important than being richer.

(e) Polar bears are vicious predators that would eat us if they could. Let them die out.

Activity 6.3

(a) To break down your research question, ask more questions, working in a group with other people who have chosen the same research question as you. Use diagrams to help you.

(b) Which of the questions you have asked are key issues? Which of them relate to information that will help you answer?

(c) What personal, national and global perspectives can you think of?

Finding information and ideas

When you are researching information and ideas, you need to think about:

- precise search terms (see page 5)
- gaps in your knowledge (see page 50).

Activity 6.4

(a) Look at each of the small questions you identified in part **(a)** of Activity 6.3.

   (i) What search terms do you need?

   (ii) Try several combinations of search terms.

(b) Look over your notes several times while you are researching and ask:

   (i) Am I finding the right balance of facts, opinions, predictions, and value judgments? If not, change the search terms.

   (ii) How do the information and ideas I am finding help me answer my question?

   (iii) Are there gaps in my knowledge? If so, how can I fill them?

Question

When you are questioning the ideas, information, and perspectives that you have found during your research, you can ask:

- How reliable is the source?
- How good is the reasoning?
- How likely are the causes and consequences?
- Are there alternative possible causes and consequences?

See pages 52–57.

Remember

Other people have personal and national perspectives too.

Make notes. Organize your notes, and keep them where you can find them.

If you have too many questions relating to facts, you can move to issues by asking: "Why do I need to know this? What consequences could come from this fact?" If you have too many questions relating to issues, you can ask: "What do I need to know to help me debate these issues?"

Remember

To decide whether an issue is important, you can consider consequences, urgency, severity, and perspectives.

Make brief, structured notes on any ideas and information you find. Keep a list of the websites you have used.

Remember

Skim-read documents for the gist before reading the relevant parts in more detail.

Make a note of which search terms are most effective for different kinds of question. Use this to make your searching skills better next time.

Activity 6.5

Almost everyone is against a noisy Diwali; most of all the intellectuals (pseudo?). For them, the bursting of crackers during Diwali is evidence of our apathy towards the environment. Our lack of concern for pollution. Noise pollution. Air pollution. Water pollution. Blah blah blah. I am not denying that the bursting of crackers causes pollution, but to suggest that this single night of revelry is anti-environment and a major cause of pollution is blatantly unfair.

Blaming firecrackers for pollution is typical of our habit of misrepresenting the truth and directing the blame in the wrong direction. The real reasons for pollution are-the CO_2-generating coal-power plants, effluent-releasing industries and petrol and diesel guzzling two- and four-wheelers. Take these out and a bulk of our problems would be solved. But do we do enough to move towards a clean environment? Do we invest heavily in nuclear power plants and in electricity-driven trains? Not at all.

Worldwide, firecrackers are the preferred way to celebrate any happy occasion. When the Olympics start or end, there is a grand show of firecrackers. When we welcome the new year in, there is a pyrotechnics show organized in many major cities – from Sydney to Singapore to even London. If all this is fine in the far more environment-conscious world, then how come it's not fine in India?

Source: http://blogs.timesofindia.indiatimes.com/the-real-truth/entry/in-support-of-a-noisy-polluting-diwali

(a) Read this extract from a blog on the website **www.timesofindia.com**
   (i) How is a blog on a newspaper website different from a personal blog?
   (ii) How reliable is this blog as a source of information? Explain your answer.

(b) The author discusses the causes of pollution. Does he suggest reasonable causes? Can you think of alternative causes that he does not mention? Explain your answer.

(c) "Take these out and a bulk of our problems would be solved." How likely is this consequence? Explain your answer.

(d) How good is the reasoning?
   (i) Are good reasons and evidence given to support the author's views?
   (ii) Can you spot emotion being used instead of reasons? Where?
   (iii) Can you spot opinions pretending to be facts?

(e) Should we address small sources of pollution even if we can't address big sources of pollution?

Activity 6.6

Look at the sources you have found so far.

(a) How reliable are they? If not very reliable, what will you do?

(b) How good is the reasoning? How will this affect the way you use the ideas, information, and perspectives in your work?

(c) How likely are the causes and consequences? If not very likely, what will you do?

(d) Are there alternative possible consequences? If so, how will this affect the way you use these ideas in your work?

> If your source is not reliable, look for a more reliable source.

> If the reasoning is poor or the consequences are unlikely, look for better-quality sources of ideas, information, and perspectives. Don't quote material that you have identified as illogical or of poor quality.

Reflect and plan

Activity 6.7

You should now have thought about climate change in some new ways.

(a) Have you thought about climate change in any new ways? If so, what and why?

(b) Have you changed your mind about anything? If so, in what way? If not, why not?

(c) Do you think that the discussion about climate change gets too emotional sometimes?

(d) How can we address climate change without harming the economy?

(e) What is the most important issue you have considered while preparing for your research report?

(f) Think of other questions to help you reflect on the issues and perspectives. Let these questions and possible answers to them float around in your mind.

(g) How does your personal perspective link with different national and global perspectives?

(h) Is your personal perspective well thought through? What evidence and reasons can you give to support your perspective?

Activity 6.8

Work in teams to plan your project.

(a) Decide on team roles, for example who will be the leader.

(b) Copy and complete the table.

Task	Who will do it	When it should be done

> Make your table as long as it needs to be for all the tasks.

Present and take action

You have now had time to reflect on the information, ideas, issues, and perspectives for your research report.

Activity 6.9

Write a research report of 500–600 words on your chosen question.
Use these headings:

- The problem

- The causes of the problem

- The consequences

- Personal, national, and global perspectives

- The possible solution
  (give your opinions here to answer the question)

Remember

When you write your research report:

▶ use your own words

▶ use clear, simple sentences

▶ give reasons to support your opinions.

Activity 6.10

Carry out your group project. Then answer these questions:

(a) What was it like working with people from another country/culture?

(b) How well did your team work together?

(c) What problems did you have?

(d) How did you solve these problems?

(e) How will you avoid these problems next time?

Section 2
7 Water, food and agriculture

Figure 7.1 How can we deal with the effects of flooding/ensure our food security?

In this chapter, you are going to work through the Global Perspectives learning process, as you did in Section 1. As you go through the process, you will practise and develop the skills you have been working on in the skills development activities for this section. You will also apply these skills as you prepare and produce a short research report and a mini project.

Research information

First you will need to think about and choose a research question and a project outcome from the suggestions in the box below.

Suggested research questions and project outcomes

(a) Choose one of these research questions.

   (i) How can we deal with the humanitarian effects of drought and flooding?

   (ii) How can we prevent conflict over water in dry areas?

   (iii) How can my country ensure its food security?

   (iv) A research question agreed with your teacher.

> **Remember**
>
> The Global Perspectives learning process:
> - ▶ Research information
> - ▶ Question
> - ▶ Reflect and plan
> - ▶ Present your findings and take action

> Why are water, food and agriculture important to humans? What effects do our uses of water and food have on other species?

> **Remember**
>
> The skills you'll learn in this section build on and develop the skills you learned in Section 1, so don't forget to use those basic skills as well.

(b) Choose one of these projects.

(i) Make a photo display of different problems associated with food or water. Explain the causes and consequences of these problems (using diagrams or a short talk).

(ii) Design a set of cartoons that illustrate the personal, national and global problems associated with food or water. Use these cartoons in a display, or to make mugs or tee-shirts to sell at a school event.

(iii) Use one of the ideas from Activity 13 in the Section 2 skills development activities (page 58) for your project.

If you are agreeing a research question with your teacher, make sure that the question allows you to look at causes, consequences, personal, national and global perspectives, and possible solutions.

If you are choosing your own project, remember to set a SMART outcome (see page 14).

Activity 7.1

Think about which research questions or project outcome you would like to try from the list of suggestions. You can use the next few activities to help you research, think and decide.

Breaking down the topic

When you break down a topic, you need to:

- ask plenty of questions and draw diagrams to show the links between them
- consider the key issues
- consider the personal, national and global perspectives.

You've already done some work on breaking down a big topic in the skills development activities in this section, on pages 43–62. Now you can apply this skill to the research question you have chosen, and break it down further into smaller questions you need to answer.

Activity 7.2

What are the personal, national and global consequences, issues, and perspectives that arise from the following?

(a) Farmers in my country aren't making money, so they are giving up on farming.

(b) It hasn't rained for 18 months in parts of Australia.

(c) A hurricane is forecast for Ohio.

(d) Storms and flooding are forecast in Bangladesh.

(e) Food shortages are leading to riots around the world.

Remember

Other people have personal and national perspectives too.

Activity 7.3

(a) To break down your research question, ask more questions, working in a group with other people who have chosen the same research question as you. Use diagrams to help you.

(b) Which of the questions you have asked are key issues? Which of them relate to information that will help you answer?

(c) What personal, national and global perspectives can you think of?

Finding information and ideas

When you are researching information and ideas, you need to think about:

- precise search terms (see page 5)
- gaps in your knowledge (see page 50).

Activity 7.4

(a) Look at each of the small questions you identified in part **(a)** of Activity 7.3.

   (i) What search terms do you need?

   (ii) Try several combinations of search terms.

(b) Look over your notes several times while you are researching and ask:

   (i) Am I finding the right balance of facts, opinions, predictions, and value judgments? If not, change your search terms.

   (ii) How do the information and ideas I am finding help me answer my question?

   (iii) Are there gaps in my knowledge? If so, how can I fill them?

Question

When you are questioning the ideas, information, and perspectives that you have found during your research, you can ask:

- How reliable is the source?
- How good is the reasoning?
- How likely are the causes and consequences?
- Are there alternative possible causes and consequences?

See pages 52–57.

> Make notes. Organize your notes, and keep them where you can find them.

> If you have too many questions relating to facts, you can move to issues by asking: "Why do I need to know this? What consequences could come from this fact?" If you have too many questions relating to issues, you can ask: "What do I need to know to help me debate these issues?"

> **Remember**
> To decide whether an issue is important, you can consider consequences, urgency, severity, and perspectives.

> Make brief, structured notes on any ideas and information you find. Keep a list of the websites you have used.

> **Remember**
> Skim-read documents for the gist before reading the relevant parts in more detail.

> Make a note of which search terms are most effective for different kinds of question. Use this to make your searching skills better next time.

The government needs to seriously consider its policies on farming and agriculture. Consumers are demanding ever-cheaper meat and milk, and supermarkets are providing these products at less than the cost of producing them. Our farmers cannot compete, so they are going out of business and we are eating imported meat and drinking imported milk. The consequences for farmers are bad enough – but if the government does not give thought to our food security, the nation could be in a disastrous position, especially if war comes.

@whoduvthoughtit: "It's only right that meat and milk are affordable. Otherwise, poor people would have nothing to eat and we'd be a poor country like Africa! Farmers should stop complaining and get on with their jobs. They're lucky to have jobs at all, or they should choose to do something else if they don't like it."

@Sweetpea: "We should take the plight of farmers more seriously. My friend's step-dad's old school friend John is a farmer, and his life is really hard. There is no money to be made and he's struggling. But he says he can't just choose another job. Farming is in his blood, and the land is part of him. And anyway, what else can he do?"

(a) How serious or sensationalist do you think the newspaper is that printed this article? Why?

(b) Do you think it is reasonable to suggest that getting much of our food from abroad will lead to bad consequences? Why (not)?

(c) Is **@whoduvthoughtit** a reliable source, in your opinion? If so, why, and if not, why not?

(d) How likely are the consequences that **@whoduvthoughtit** suggests? Explain your answer.

(e) How good is **@whoduvthoughtit's** reasoning? Explain your answer.

(f) **@Sweetpea** refers to her "friend's step-dad's old school friend John". How reliable is this source? Explain your answer.

(g) Is **@Sweetpea** providing reasons to support an opinion? Explain your answer.

Look at the sources you have found so far.

(a) How reliable are they? If not very reliable, what will you do?

(b) How reliable is the reasoning? How will this affect the way you use the ideas, information and perspectives in your work?

(c) How likely are the causes and consequences? If not, what will you do?

(d) Are there alternative possible consequences? If so, how will this affect the way you use these ideas in your work?

> If your source is not reliable, look for a more reliable source.

> If the reasoning is poor or the consequences are unlikely, look for better-quality sources of ideas, information, and perspectives. Don't quote material that you have identified as illogical or of poor quality.

Reflect and plan

Activity 7.7

You should now have thought about water, food and agriculture in some new ways.

(a) Have you thought about water food and agriculture in any new ways? If so, what and why?

(b) Have you changed your mind about anything? Why (not)?

(c) Do you think that milk and meat should be cheap, even if farmers struggle to make a living?

(d) How far do you think our upbringing and job (like farming) becomes a part of who we are?

(e) What is the most important issue you have considered while preparing your research report?

(f) Think of other questions to help you reflect on the issues and perspectives. Let these questions and possible answers to them float around in your mind.

(g) How does your personal perspective link with different national and global perspectives?

(h) Is your personal perspective well thought through? What evidence and reasons can you give to support your perspective?

Activity 7.8

Work in teams to plan your project.

(a) Decide on team roles, for example who will be the leader.

(b) Copy and complete the table.

Task	Who will do it	When it should be done

Make your table as long as it needs to be for all the tasks.

Present and take action

You have now had time to reflect on the information, ideas, issues, and perspectives for your research report.

Activity 7.9

Write a research report of 500–600 words on your chosen question. Use these headings:

- The problem
- The causes of the problem
- The consequences
- Personal, national and global perspectives
- The possible solution
  (give your opinions here to answer the question)

Remember

When you write your research report:

▶ use your own words

▶ use clear, simple sentences

▶ give reasons to support your opinions.

Activity 7.10

Carry out your group project. Then answer these questions:

(a) What was it like working with people from another country/culture?

(b) How well did your team work together?

(c) What problems did you have?

(d) How did you solve these problems?

(e) How will you avoid these problems next time?

Section 2
8 Fuel and energy

Figure 8.1 What kinds of fuel should we use for our energy supply?

In this chapter, you are going to work through the Global Perspectives learning process, as you did in Section 1. As you go through the process, you will practise and develop the skills you have been working on in the Skills development activities for this section. You will also apply these skills as you prepare and produce a short research report and a mini project.

Research information

First you will need to think about and choose a research question and a project outcome from the suggestions in the box below.

Suggested research questions and project outcomes

(a) Choose one of these research questions.

(i) What kinds of fuel should governments invest in for the future?

(ii) How reasonable is it for nations to keep using oil, even though this contributes to climate change?

(iii) How can individuals contribute to national efforts to reduce fuel use?

(iv) A research question agreed with your teacher.

Why are fuel and energy important to humans? What effects do our uses of fuel and energy have on other species?

(b) Choose one of these projects.

> **(i)** Make a photo display of different problems associated with fuel and energy. Explain the causes and consequences of these problems (using diagrams or a short talk).
>
> **(ii)** Design a set of cartoons that illustrate the personal, national and global problems associated with fuel and energy. Use these cartoons in a display, or to make mugs or T-shirts to sell at a school event.
>
> **(iii)** Use one of the ideas from Activity 13 in the Section 2 skills development activities (page 58) for your project.

> If you are agreeing a research question with your teacher, make sure that the question allows you to look at causes, consequences, personal, national and global perspectives, and possible solutions.

> If you are choosing your own project, remember to set a SMART outcome (see page 14).

Activity 8.1

Think about which research questions or project outcome you would like to try from the list of suggestions. You can use the next few activities to help you research, think and decide.

Breaking down the topic

When you break down a topic, you need to:

- ask plenty of questions and draw diagrams to show the links between them
- consider the key issues
- consider the personal, national and global perspectives.

> Biomass power is fueled by burning organic materials, such as wood from trees.

You've already done some work on breaking down a big topic in the skills development activities in this section, on pages 43–62. Now you can apply this skill to the research question you have chosen, and break it down further into smaller questions you need to answer.

Activity 8.2

What are the personal, national and global consequences, issues and perspectives that arise from the following?

(a) There is significant opposition to a biomass power station planned for the docks.

(b) Wind turbines will ruin the view.

(c) It's raining so I'll drive to work.

(d) It would be wonderful to have electricity in our village.

(e) Why should I cut down my fuel use when big industries are using more and more?

Activity 8.3

(a) To break down your research question, ask more questions, working in a group with other people who have chosen the same research question as you. Use diagrams to help you.

(b) Which of the questions you have asked are key issues? Which of them relate to information that will help you answer?

(c) What personal, national and global perspectives can you think of?

Finding information and ideas

When you are researching information and ideas, you need to think about:

● precise search terms (see page 5)

● gaps in your knowledge (see page 50).

Activity 8.4

(a) Look at each of the small questions you identified in Activity 8.3, part **(a)**.

    (i) What search terms do you need?

    (ii) Try several combinations of search terms.

(b) Look over your notes several times while you are researching and ask:

    (i) Am I finding the right balance of facts, opinions, predictions, and value judgments? If not, change your search terms.

    (ii) How do the information and ideas I am finding help me answer my question?

    (iii) Are there gaps in my knowledge? If so, how can I fill them?

Question

When you are questioning the ideas, information, and perspectives that you have found during your research, you can ask:

● How reliable is this source?

● How good is the reasoning?

● How likely are the causes and consequences?

● Are there alternative possible causes and consequences?

See pages 52–57.

Remember

Other people have personal and national perspectives too.

Make notes. Organize your notes, and keep them where you can find them.

If you have too many questions relating to facts, you can move to issues by asking: "Why do I need to know this? What consequences could come from this fact?" If you have too many questions relating to issues, you can ask: "What do I need to know to help me debate these issues?"

Remember

To decide whether an issue is important, you can consider consequences, urgency, severity, and perspectives.

Make brief, structured notes on any ideas and information you find. Keep a list of the websites you have used.

Remember

Skim-read documents for the gist before reading the relevant parts in more detail.

Make a note of which search terms are most effective for different kinds of question. Use this to make your searching skills better next time.

Activity 8.5

Energy companies have announced plans to build or convert power stations which altogether would burn 81 million tonnes of wood every year. The UK's total wood production (for all purposes) is only 10 million tonnes annually. Planning consent has been granted for five coal-power stations to partly or fully convert to wood. Those power stations alone will burn almost five times the UK's annual wood production every year.

Not surprisingly then, 80 per cent of biomass is expected to be imported. Most imports so far are from British Columbia and the southern US, two regions where highly biodiverse and carbon-rich forests are being clearcut at an ever faster rate. And one scientific study after another confirms that burning trees for electricity results in vast carbon emissions, which cannot possibly be absorbed by new trees for decades or centuries, if ever. So the government's renewable energy strategy will continue to make climate change, deforestation and air pollution ever worse.

Source: http://www.redpepper.org.uk/biomass-the-trojan-horse-of-renewables/

(a) Read the extract and then look up redpepper.org.uk. How reliable is this as a source of information? Explain your answer.

(b) The article predicts that "80 per cent of biomass is expected to be imported". How likely is this consequence? Explain your answer.

(c) The article concludes that "the government's renewable energy strategy will continue to make climate change, deforestation and air pollution ever worse".

   (i) How likely is this consequence? Explain your answer.

   (ii) Are good reasons and evidence given to support this conclusion? Go to the original article on www. biofuelwatch. org, and click on the link to the scientific studies.

(d) What alternative forms of renewable energy can you think of? Would they have better consequences in your opinion than biomass?

> If your source is unreliable, look for a more reliable source.

Activity 8.6

Look at the sources you have found so far.

(a) How reliable are they? If they are not very reliable, what will you do?

(b) Is the reasoning generally good quality? How will this affect the way you use the ideas, information, and perspectives in your work?

(c) How likely are the causes and consequences? If they are not very likely, what will you do?

(d) Are there alternative possible consequences? If so, how will this affect the way you use these ideas in your work?

Reflect and plan

Activity 8.7

You should now have thought about fuel and energy in some new ways.

(a) Have you thought about fuel and energy in any new ways? If so, what and why?

(b) Have you changed your mind about anything? If so, in what way? If not, why not?

(c) Do you think that more resources should be put into finding renewable energy?

(d) How can we all reduce our energy use without harming the economy?

(e) What is the most important issue you have considered while preparing for your research report?

(f) Think of other questions to help you reflect on the issues and perspectives. Let these questions and possible answers to them float around in your mind.

(g) How does your personal perspective link with different national and global perspectives?

(h) Is your personal perspective well thought through? What evidence and reasons can you give to support your perspective?

> If the reasoning is poor or the consequences are unlikely, look for better-quality sources of ideas, information, and perspectives. Don't quote material that you have identified as illogical or of poor quality.

Activity 8.8

Work in teams to plan your project.

(a) Decide on team roles, for example who will be the leader.

(b) Copy and complete the table.

Task	Who will do it	When it should be done

> Make your table as long as it needs to be for all the tasks.

Present and take action

You have now had time to reflect on the information, ideas, issues, and perspectives for your research report.

Activity 8.9

Write a research report of 500–600 words on your chosen question. Use these headings:

- The problem

- The causes of the problem

- The consequences

- Personal, national and global perspectives

- The possible solution
  (give your opinions here to answer the question)

Activity 8.10

Carry out your group project. Then answer these questions:

(a) What was it like working with people from another country/culture?

(b) How well did your team work together?

(c) What problems did you have?

(d) How did you solve these problems?

(e) How will you avoid these problems next time?

Section 3
Skills development activities

In this section, you will be developing your skills further, revising and extending the skills you worked on in Sections 1 and 2. You'll apply these skills more independently and will work on a full-length individual research report and group project. You'll start thinking about assessment requirements.

In this section, you'll practise the skills through consideration of these topics:

● Transport and infrastructure

● Urbanization

● Disease and health

● Poverty and inequality

Research information

Researching information for a individual research report or group project is not *only* about collecting as much information as you can find. It's also about using this information selectively to plan a line of inquiry. How do you decide just what information is relevant and is going to be useful?

First, you will need to:

● focus on a small part of the bigger topic

● set a relevant question to answer.

Then you will be able to evaluate the information, ideas and perspectives you have researched and select only the items that will help you answer the question.

It's like panning for gold or sapphires. You need to know where you are likely to find the gold or sapphires and you need to be able to tell the difference between the valuable nuggets and the worthless stones.

"Help! I don't know anything about infrastructure/urbanization/disease/poverty. How will I know what's relevant if I don't know anything? How do I even start?"

Activity 1

How do I start?

To help you get started, think about the following questions:

(a) How can you use the skills you developed in Sections 1 and 2 to start searching for relevant and interesting ideas, information and perspectives?

(b) What do you know already that could help you?

(c) Is there something that you know you don't know - a gap in your knowledge that you can identify? If so, how could you use this to help you get started?

Focusing on a small part of the topic

Once you have made a start, it's fairly easy to find lots of information on the Internet. In fact, there can be too much! In order to choose a small part of the bigger topic, you have to break the topic down. This is easiest if you organize it in your head. Try asking these questions:

You could also ask:

"What is being done already? How effective is it?"

- What are the key issues?
- What are the personal, national and global problems and perspectives?
- What are the main problems in this area?
- What are the possibilities?
- How does this link with what I already know?
- Which bits are the most interesting?

Use these questions to guide your search for information. When you find information, try to classify it. Is it a key issue, unimportant, or quite important but not really key? Is it a personal, national, or global issue? Is it a problem, as solution, or neither? Is it interesting enough to research more?

Activity 2

The following table shows two big topics, infrastructure and urbanization, broken down into some of their key issues.

Infrastructure	Urbanization
Infrastructure and economic development	Effects on food and farming
Ageing infrastructure	Quality of life and the environment, e.g. housing, privacy, noise, open space, sky, facilities
Infrastructure and the environment/climate	Nature of work
Specific infrastructure projects, e.g. the Three Gorges Dam or a new airport	Investment in employment
Paying for infrastructure	Infrastructure needed
Infrastructure necessary for your own particular interest. Problems, e.g. personal vs global	Effects on the environment/climate

(a) Which issues do you find the most interesting?

(b) Is there an issue you find interesting that hasn't been mentioned?

(c) What links can you see between the issues?

(d) Choose one issue and formulate a question about it.

Setting a relevant question

To help you decide what information you need and how valuable it will be for your topic, you need to have a relevant question about that topic. Once you have formulated your question, you can start to plan how you will develop your inquiry. Use the questions in the list at the top of this page to help you.

You may change your question a bit as you research and think more. But you still need to think of a question to help you focus your research and thinking.

A good question will:

- give you focus
- require you to develop a line of reasoning (this means justifying your opinions and values, not just describing)
- help you meet the assessment requirements, including looking at problems, their causes and consequences, possible solutions, and different perspectives.

Why is a question important?

If you simply give your individual research report a name, such as "**The Three Gorges Dam**", it won't give you focus since it is not a question. It won't help you develop a line of inquiry, and it won't help you meet the assessment requirements. This is merely an invitation for you to write down everything you know about a topic without organizing it or thinking about it.

However, if you ask a question instead, such as "**In the long term, is the Three Gorges Dam likely to be beneficial overall?**" it will give you a focus. It will make you develop a line of reasoning, because you have to form an opinion and justify it. It will help you meet the assessment requirements, because you will have to predict consequences and weigh up the positive and negative perspectives. The question asks you to think of solutions to some of the existing problems, and to consider the personal and global impacts.

Then you can test all the information you research against your question, according to the following flow chart.

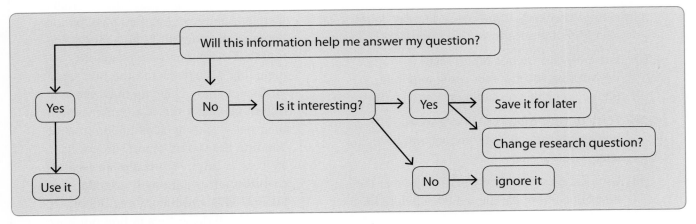

Figure 1 Testing the relevance of information

Activity 3

(a) Look at these questions. Will they help you focus, develop reasoning and meet the assessment criteria?

   (i) What are the key issues in poverty and inequality?

   (ii) Should we build a new airport in my area?

   (iii) What is the quality of life like in Delhi?

   (iv) What are the effects of urbanization on people's quality of life? How can we deal with these effects?

   (v) How can we ensure that all children are vaccinated against serious diseases?

(b) Go back through the area you chose for part **(d)** of Activity 2. Write a question to help you plan your inquiry.

Evaluating what you find

Whenever you do research, you need to evaluate what you find. Remember to keep using the skills you learned in Sections 1 and 2 as well as the new skills from this section. In this section, you will learn about:

- cross-checking facts
- more ways of evaluating predicted consequences.

Cross-checking facts

You learned in Section 2 how to make a judgment about the reliability and credibility of a source. But you also need to cross-check the facts with other sources, to make sure they are correct. Sometimes a reliable source can make a mistake, or an unreliable source may get a statistic right.

- Put a fact or statistic into a search engine to see if other sources agree with it.
- Make sure that you find reliable, credible sources when you are cross-checking facts.
- Check where these sources found their information, and whether that is reliable.

Activity 4

(a) Do you think the following facts have been sufficiently checked? What other sources could you check? What questions could you ask?

  (i) Forty of your friends on a social networking site say that using a mobile phone can give you brain cancer.

  (ii) Forty of your friends say on a social networking site that the school will be closed due to snow.

  (iii) You read on a social networking site that the new Pope has to eat the old Pope before he can become Pope. You do an Internet search and find many newspaper results saying, "The new Pope eats with the old Pope."

  (iv) A newspaper article claims that 2 billion people live on less than $1 a day. You believe it.

  (v) A newspaper claims that "the 100 richest people in the world earned $240 billion between them in 2012". You check, and find that many news organizations, including Al Jazeera and the BBC, quote an Oxfam study claiming that "the 100 richest people in the world increased their net wealth by $240 billion in 2012". You find the Oxfam report. It cites its sources as **http://www.globalresearch.ca/billionaires-gain-as-living-standards-fall/5318471** and Bloomberg Billionaires. You look up these sites to find out how they arrived at the figure.

(b) cross-check the facts given in parts **(a) (i)** and **(a) (iv)**.

Checking facts, evaluating opinions, predictions and value judgments

When you are cross-checking, think about the difference between facts, opinions, predictions, and value judgments. Remember that you can verify a fact. You can't verify opinions, predictions or value judgments, but you can evaluate how well supported, likely or reasonable they are. For example:

- "72% of men are over 1.75 m tall." If it's true, this is a **fact**. You can check this with several sources to verify it – or establish that it is false.

- "Tall people are superior to short people." This is an **opinion** (or prejudice) that cannot be checked or verified. Instead of verifying them, you can consider whether opinions are well supported with reasons and evidence.

- "Vaccinating all children will save a million lives." This is a **prediction**, and since it hasn't happened yet it can't be verified. Instead, you can think about how likely it is to happen.

- "It is wrong to let people die of curable diseases." This is a **value judgment**, so it can't be verified. Instead, you can evaluate it by thinking about how reasonable it is, and testing it against other perspectives.

Beware of opinions that are made to look like facts. Just because a statement includes a number or statistic, it doesn't mean it's a fact.

"The world's 100 richest people could end hunger." This has a number in it, but it is not a fact. It's an opinion based on predictions and facts. "The world's 100 richest people increased their wealth by $240 billion in 2012" is a fact that can be verified. But whether they could use this amount of money to end hunger depends on other things. You can ask questions such as:

- How would the money be used?

- Would they pay for one year of food for everyone? What about the next year?

- Would they help people develop businesses? What if these businesses fail?

- What if there is another drought?

Evaluating consequences

In Section 2, you started to evaluate the likeliness of a consequence. Now you're going to think about some more ways of evaluating how realistic and likely a predicted consequence is. If you make a decision based on an exaggerated prediction of the consequences, it is likely to be a poor decision.

Activity 5

Which of the following are facts that can be verified?

(i) Eighty per cent of people live on less than $10 a day

(ii) Living in a rural area is better than living in a city.

(iii) It is wrong to cure sick people who can't afford to look after themselves.

(iv) Eighty per cent of poverty is due to laziness.

(v) Building the new airport will generate $3 million for the economy.

Watch out for these kinds of unrealistic predictions of consequences:

- Exaggeration
- Oversimplification
- Ignoring other possibilities

Watch out for unrealistic predictions of consequences in your own work, as well as in sources you find during research.

Exaggeration

When people are predicting consequences, they often exaggerate. They overstate the possible consequences of an action. This can be either wishful thinking or disaster thinking.

Wishful thinking is too positive, seeing things as better than they could possibly be. For example:

> "If we vaccinate every child, we can wipe out disease and sickness, and everyone will grow up healthy and happy and have an economically productive life."

This prediction overstates the positive aspects of vaccination so much that it is unrealistic. Even if we vaccinated every child in the world, we might succeed in wiping out the diseases we have vaccinated against (or they may mutate and come back in a different form) but we certainly won't wipe out disease and sickness totally, because we can't vaccinate against all illnesses. Even with vaccination, children often get a milder form of the sickness, so vaccinating every child won't wipe out sickness and disease. Furthermore, other things contribute to health, happiness, and economic productivity, not just vaccination. Accidents, poor nutrition and family troubles, for example, can affect all of these.

As you see, this predicted consequence is exaggerated. But vaccinating every child might still be a good idea. You'd need to take a more realistic look at the possible consequences.

Disaster thinking is too negative, seeing things as worse than they are ever likely to be. For example:

> "If any more people move into the city, the city just won't be able to cope. The slum areas will grow, there will be piles of human waste lying around, people will get sick and die, the gangs will recruit poor people who can't get work, and they will attack the rich and take over power and it will end up being a lawless anarchy."

More people moving into cities from the country (or other parts of the world) can lead to problems, but this reasoning overstates them. It is possible that *some* more people could move into the city before everything collapses. Perhaps not all the people who move in will be poor or unskilled. While overcrowding in poor parts of a city *can* lead to problems with sanitation and health, many cities still cope without piles of human waste lying around. Gangs do sometimes recruit the poor, but gangs taking over an entire city is less common.

As you see, the consequences predicted here are too extreme.

Oversimplification

Most of the contexts in Global Perspectives are complex, with multiple causes and consequences. We have to simplify them in order to make sense of them. But if we make decisions based on *over*simplified predictions, they are likely to be poor decisions. For example:

> "Poverty means having no money. If we give poor people money, we will solve poverty."

This reasoning is oversimplified. It ignores the many causes of poverty, and the many different forms of poverty. If people are to escape from poverty, they need to make wise decisions about spending and investing money. To truly not be poor, people need access to education, health services, and good food. Furthermore, if we give people money but make them dependent, we might be trapping them into a different kind of poverty.

Ignoring other possibilities

Sometimes people predict a consequence that is possible, but ignore other possible consequences. This can lead to poor decision making too. For example:

> "If we build a factory, there will be work for the people."

This seems to be a reasonable consequence. But there may be other consequences – will the factory use the water that farmers rely on to irrigate their crops? Will the factory provide additional work, or will it replace better jobs that were already there? Will the factory change the social and economic structure of the local area by employing mostly women? Will the repayments on the loan for the factory be more than the money the factory makes? Will the factory damage the environment? Will the factory have health implications for the local population? All of these possible consequences (and more) need to be considered before a decision is made about building a factory.

> Sometimes exaggeration, oversimplification and ignoring other possibilities can seem similar to one another – or a statement may have done all these things at once. Remember to explain why you think a predicted consequence would be unrealistic or unlikely, and suggest other possibilities.

Activity 6

Explain why the following predictions are unrealistic or unlikely, and suggest other possibilities.

(i) If we build a new ring road, the traffic will get very much better. This will bring more business to the city and should generate about $4 million in new revenue.

(ii) If I borrow $1 million to invest in my business, I'll create employment for many local people.

(iii) The government should set up a regional development agency. This will stop people from migrating to the cities.

(iv) Donating money to help prevent malaria is pointless. These people will only make dresses out of the mosquito nets instead of using them to protect their children.

Future actions

When you've analysed and evaluated a problem, you need to think about future actions – what can be done to solve the problem or make the situation better? These could be personal or local decisions; simple actions that individuals and communities might take; government policy; or international action. Maybe a combination of personal, national and global actions is necessary.

You'll need to evaluate possible future actions by:

- considering who can or should take action
- thinking about the likely consequences of these actions
- weighing up positive and negative consequences.

Let's look at an example:

A: You feel unwell. You are not sure whether you have the flu. Should you stay at home or go to school for exam practice?

This is a personal decision. You need to balance your health and your education, and consider the risk of infecting others.

B: There is a flu epidemic in your country. Should schools stay open during the exam period?

This is now a decision for school management or maybe even the government. The importance of education and good exam results needs to be weighed against the importance of health for the country.

Activity 7

Your school is depressing and grey. The buildings are old, there are cracks in the walls and the paint is peeling. The computers are 20th century and the science labs are 19th century. The toilets are always disgusting, and there is litter everywhere. There is an increasing problem with bad behaviour.

List the appropriate actions that each of the following groups of people could take to improve the situation.

Could any other groups of people take action? For every action you think of, consider the consequences.

- Students
- Teachers
- Management
- Parents
- The government
- The United Nations

Reflect and plan

How do I reflect?

Reflection is a kind of quiet thinking, when you bring information and ideas together, looking for patterns, connections, implications and meaning. It's about weighing up all the evaluative thinking you've done.

Different people have different ways of reflecting. Some people write and think, others paint and think. Some people find that walking in a calm

place helps them sort out their thoughts. Albus Dumbledore, Headmaster of Hogwarts in *Harry Potter and the Goblet of Fire*, uses a pensieve:

> "One simply siphons the excess thoughts from one's mind, pours them into the basin, and examines them at one's leisure. It becomes easier to spot patterns and links, you understand, when they are in this form."

Reflection should help you make sense of an issue, decide what your opinion is and think about what would be the best actions to take.

Activity 8

(a) Since you don't have a pensieve (unless you are, in fact, a witch or wizard…), what strategies can you use to help you examine your thoughts? What can you do to help yourself spot patterns and links? Share ideas with your classmates.

(b) Section 3 deals with four topics: Transport and infrastructure, Urbanization, Disease and health, and Poverty and inequality. You will study one of these topics in detail later. For now, use a mind map to help you reflect on the links between them. For example:

"Poor sanitation (infrastructure) causes disease causes poverty causes migration to the city (urbanization) causes poor sanitation…"

Project planning

Project planning is about taking the ideas from your research, questioning, and reflection and using them in the real world to make a difference. You have thought about various possible decisions, actions and policies that might solve a problem, and considered the consequences of these actions. Now you need to work in a team to:

- choose an appropriate action (outcome) based on your research and thinking
- plan the tasks that need to be done
- carry out the action
- evaluate the effectiveness of your action.

Choosing an action or outcome

Remember that when you choose an action or outcome, it needs to be SMART. For Global Perspectives, your action or outcome also needs to:

- show that you have researched and thought about an issue
- allow you to show understanding of personal, national, global and cross-cultural perspectives
- involve local actions that reflect national and global issues (after all, you don't have the same resources as the government or the World Health Organization!)
- allow you to collaborate with people from another culture, community, or country.

Activity 9

Think about the following possible actions. Are they suitable for a Global Perspectives project? Explain your reasoning in terms of research and thinking, different perspectives, appropriate actions, and collaboration.

(a) Cleaning a local river, together with members of the community

(b) Organizing a project to vaccinate children in a village in Malawi

(c) Raising funds to support a charity that vaccinates children in Malawi

(d) Making a poster about poverty

(e) Producing a video campaigning for or against a local infrastructure project

(f) Writing a research report on urbanization.

Remember

SMART outcomes are **S**pecific, **M**easurable, **A**chievable, **R**ealistic and **T**ime-bound.

The project planning process

Let's look at the processes involved in planning and managing a project with an active outcome. As an example, we'll be looking at organizing a music concert to raise awareness of an issue you have studied. Important things to remember are:

- A project is about managing practical tasks as well as research tasks.
- A project deals with teamwork and people as well as information.
- You need to be prepared to review and amend your plan.

You can think of the project process like this:

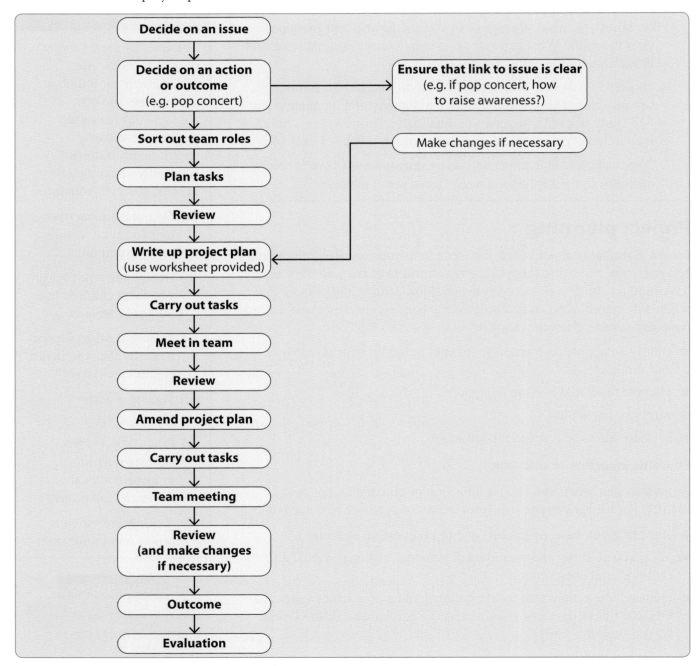

Figure 2 The project process

Some of the questions you can ask yourself at different stages of the project process include the following:

Stage	Questions to ask
Deciding on the issue	Does your teacher give you the issue?
	Do you choose it?
Deciding on the action or outcome	Is it SMART?
	Is it appropriate local action showing understanding of different perspectives?
	How will you collaborate with another culture, community, or country?
Sorting out team roles	Who is the leader or will you rotate that role?
	Who is the issue researcher?
	Who is liaising with other groups?
	How rigid will the roles be?
Planning tasks	What will the concert be like?
	Will you have internationally famous bands, local bands, school bands or team members singing (badly)?
	How will the concert raise awareness of the issue?
	What needs to be done?
	Who is doing which task?
	When does each task need to be done?
	Do some tasks need to be done before others can start?
	Do you need to revise team roles?
Review	Is the outcome possible or realistic
	Is the plan realistic? Can you really get an international band?
	How is your concert going to raise awareness?
	How will the concert (or write-up of the concert) represent the cross-cultural collaboration?
	Are the tasks fairly shared out?
	Are you playing to your team's strengths?
	Have you thought of everything that needs to be done? Who is booking the stage? What about money? What about publicity?
Team meeting	Check on progress, review, and make changes.
	What difficulties are you facing? How can these be solved?
Review	Are all team members working well?
	How will you deal with those who are not working well?
	Are the workloads fair?

Stage	Questions to ask
	Do you need to add some more tasks? Who should do them?
	How well is your team communicating?
	How will you solve problems?
Outcome	How do you document the outcome?
	Do you need photos or a video to demonstrate that your concert really took place?
	How will your documentation show your thinking about the issue?
	How will your documentation show your understanding of different perspectives?
	How will your documentation show your cross-cultural collaboration?
Evaluation	Did you achieve your aims?
	If not, why not?
	How well did you work within the team?

Activity 10

(a) How can you make a concert relevant to your chosen issue (poverty/health/urbanization/ infrastructure)?

(b) What practical ways can you think of to make sure that the pop concert really does raise awareness of the issue?

(c) Make a list of everything you will need to organize your concert.

(d) Make a list of everything you will need to do to organize your concert.

Present your findings and act on them

Developing a line of reasoning

When you are presenting the results of your research and thinking, it isn't enough to write down lists of information and ideas. You need to:

● use the ideas and evidence to help you answer a question or decide on a course of action

● organize and structure your thoughts into a line of reasoning.

How do I organize my thoughts into a line of reasoning?

● Write lists of reasons for and against your opinion/conclusion/proposal.

● Think about "mini" conclusions that come between your reasons and final opinion/conclusion/proposal.

● Think about evidence and examples to support and illustrate the reasons. This is usually where you can quote your research evidence.

● Use words like *because, so, therefore, also, furthermore,* to link your ideas.

- Before you start writing, you need to know what your final opinion, conclusion, or proposal for action is. If you're not sure, go back to the Reflect and plan stage!

You can draw a tree diagram to help you:

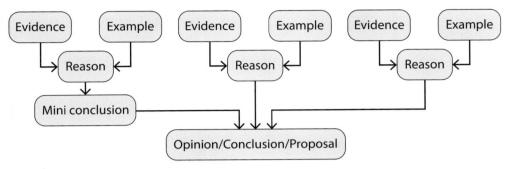

Figure 3 Organizing thoughts into a line of reasoning

Let's look at an example. How well do the responses A and B below answer this question?

> "Should I donate to a charity that aims to vaccinate all children against common childhood diseases?"

A: One to two doses of a US$0.14 vaccine could prevent a disease that affects practically the whole population of Sub-Saharan Africa and that has an approximate case-fatality rate of 3 to 6 per cent. Vaccines are one of the most equitable, low-cost, high-impact public health measures. Diptheria, cholera, typhoid, malaria, measles and polio is all disises that can kill childrens. Poliovirus is most often transmitted fecal-orally from person to person in unsanitary and crowded conditions.

Comment: This response does not answer the question. It just gives information about vaccines and diseases without organization, structure, or thought. Furthermore, most of this information is plagiarized: it has been cut and pasted from another source without reference. (We can tell this because a candidate who writes, '... is all disises that can kill childrens,' has a fairly low level of English and is unlikely to write "transmitted fecal-orally...")

B: Vaccines are a good way of spending money **because** they are a cheap, fair and effective way of saving lives and improving health. *This is shown by* http://www.ncbi.nlm.nih.gov/books/NBK2284/, "One to two doses of a US$0.14 vaccine could prevent a disease that affects practically the whole population of Sub-Saharan Africa with an approximate case-fatality rate of 3 to 6 per cent." It matters to me that people have the chance at good health, **because** health is really important for living a happy and productive life. I *also* believe that it's wrong that people should die of preventable diseases. **Therefore** I should donate some money to the charity.

Comment: This response does answer the question. It's also well structured (if not perfect!). It uses evidence and personal values, which are both important in making a personal decision about spending money. You could make a tree diagram of this answer.

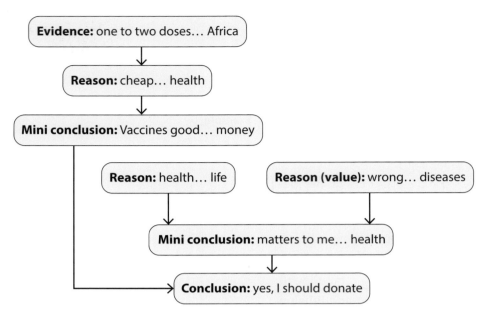

Figure 4 Structuring an answer

Causes, consequences, and possible solutions

Another way to structure your reasoning is to put your reasons into categories. These categories may be the causes or consequences of the problem you are thinking about, or they may be the possible solutions to the problem, or the predicted consequences of a possible solution:

Activity 11

For each of the following conclusions, write down any reasons, evidence, examples, and mini conclusions. Use a tree diagram like the one on the left to plan your line of reasoning.

(a) We should build a new airport here.

(b) The government should invest in rural areas to prevent migration to the city.

(c) Giving people food does not help to end poverty.

(d) The best way to improve health is to improve sanitation.

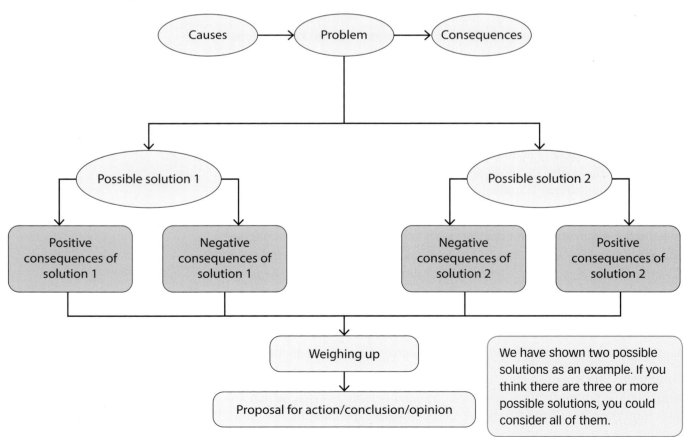

We have shown two possible solutions as an example. If you think there are three or more possible solutions, you could consider all of them.

Figure 5 Structuring an answer using a mind map

Activity 12

Choose one conclusion from Activity 11. Categorize your reasons into causes, consequences, possible solutions, and consequences of possible solutions. Use a mind map like the one in Figure 5. Can you think of any more reasons now?

Perspectives

Problems, causes, consequences, and possible solutions can be personal, national, or global. Another way to structure your reasoning is by thinking in terms of these perspectives.

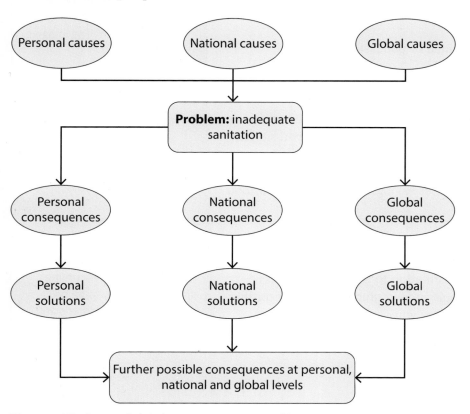

Figure 6 Mind map of global perspectives on a problem

Activity 13

Choose one conclusion from Activity 11. Categorize the causes, consequences, and problems in terms of personal, national, and global perspectives and further possible consequences. Use a mind map like the one in Figure 6.

(a) Can personal solutions ever have global consequences? Think of examples.

(b) Can global solutions ever have personal consequences? Think of examples.

Logical thinking

We have talked about some ways to organize your thoughts. As well as having a structure, however, you also need to use logical thinking and to make connections between the different parts of your argument. Without them, your reasoning is empty – like a house with no people living in it.

Multimedia presentations

It is often most effective to mix writing with other media when you are presenting your reasoning, conclusions, and proposals. For components 1 and 2 of the Global Perspectives assessment, you are allowed to provide multimedia presentations, both for your individual research report and the group report on your project. This means that you can back up your writing with:

- recorded speech, in the form of a video or podcast
- images, in the form of posters, diagrams or photographs
- a PowerPoint presentation

> Use and refer to multimedia. Avoid long descriptions - your audience can see the image. For example, "The image demonstrates/ implies…" is much better than "The image is of two children."

Whichever of these media you choose, the most important point is to ensure that it is relevant. Include videos, images, diagrams etc. to help you support your overall conclusion or proposal, and make sure that you use and refer to them. Show or tell the audience how they help to answer your question or support a proposal. This can be as simple as saying "as Figure 1/the cartoon shows…".

Speaking clearly

If you are going to record speech, it must be clear and easy to hear. This is true whether you are recording a presentation to the school or class, making a video of interviews with people in your community, or recording a team meeting for your project. Make sure you:

- speak clearly and slowly so that your audience can understand you
- use good-quality recording equipment.

> Background noise can be very distracting. Avoid recording if there are likely to be bells, banging doors, footsteps and loud voices.

Here are some tips for speaking well:

- Speak in your own words. Do not read. Reading makes you mumble and it is boring for your audience.
- Make sure you understand everything you are saying. If what you are saying is too complicated for you, it will be too complicated for your audience.
- Choose two to four key points to make. Make these important points interesting but keep them simple. You can't say everything.
- Vary your tone and speed to make what you say even more interesting.

Speaking in public is scary. It is especially scary if English is not your first language. Be confident, don't worry about mistakes and keep practising. It will help if you:

- smile
- use eye contact

- use gestures
- use images to back up what you are saying (see below).

Form two teams and play these games to make you more confident about speaking without reading.

(a) Write 30–60 everyday words, such as egg, sheep, sky, on separate cards. Put the cards in a bag. Person 1 chooses a card and speaks about it for 30 seconds. Person 2 pulls out a card and speaks about it for 30 seconds, making a link between the first word and the second word. Person 3 pulls out a card and speaks, making links between all three words. The links can be funny or serious. How many people can speak before it becomes too difficult? Can Team 2 do better than Team 1?

(b) Prepare 20–30 cards with key words from the Section 3 topics, such as sanitation, vaccination, airport. Put the cards in a bag. Each team takes out a card. You have one minute to prepare, everyone must say at least one sentence, and you must:

(i) mention a problem related to the word

(ii) consider at least one cause of the problem

(iii) discuss one consequence

(iv) speak without reading.

You could also:

(v) suggest one possible solution

(vi) say whether you think this is a good solution, and why

(vii) video yourself and the other members of your team speaking. Watch the video to see whether you are speaking clearly and slowly, making eye contact and using gestures.

Using images

Images should always be relevant and have a purpose. Always ask yourself, 'What is this image here for?' If it's just for decoration, get rid of it and find something that:

- is relevant
- illustrates your point
- helps your audience understand what you are writing or saying
- shows a thought process (e.g. a mind map or flow chart)
- conveys an idea to your audience (e.g. a diagram or photo)
- is amusing as well as relevant (e.g. a cartoon).

Then ask yourself, "Have I <u>used</u> this image and referred to it?" If not, do so!

Using posters

Like images, posters should be relevant and have a purpose. They are mainly visual ways of showing ideas. A good poster will have mainly images – such as photos, cartoons, flow charts, mind maps, and diagrams – and a few words too. Use words sparingly, though – would you read a poster that was all words?

When you are making a poster, think about what you want it to achieve.

Using PowerPoint

When people give presentations, they often use PowerPoint software to help them. PowerPoint can be a wonderful tool, which combines images, video, audio and key words. On the other hand, a badly produced PowerPoint makes for a really dull talk. People often make the mistake of putting a whole essay on their slides, in tiny writing, and then reading it out word for word without even looking at the audience... that's only good for an afternoon snooze at the back of the room!

Here are some tips for using PowerPoint effectively:

- Organize and structure your thinking very clearly on paper before you start.

- Make two to four key points only.

- Write one heading on each slide, followed by – at most – two or three bullet points.

- Use a font size that everyone in the room will be able to read.

- Use relevant images – for example, diagrams showing causes and consequences, mind maps showing personal, national and global perspectives, images that support what you are saying, and cartoons that show key issues.

- Keep the slides simple so that they aren't distracting your audience from your message.

- Speak clearly, without reading.

Activity 15

Produce a multimedia presentation. Choose one of the following:

(a) Support (or disagree with) one of the conclusions from Activity 11.

(b) Answer the question you wrote in part **(b)** of Activity 3.

Remember

Structure your ideas so that they are clear, relevant, and focused.

Section 3
9 Transport and infrastructure

If you do decide to submit work from this section for assessment, come back and check it again after you have worked through Sections 4 and 5.

In Sections 1 and 2, you produced practice research reports and projects. Now you will be producing full-length work which could be submitted for assessment. You will also be doing activities that will enable you to practise the skills you need and help you prepare for the kinds of question that you may find in the written paper.

Research information

What is infrastructure?

Infrastructure: The basic systems and equipment needed for a country, region, or organization to function.

Suggested research questions and project outcomes

(a) Choose one of these research questions.

   (i) Choose a major infrastructure project in your country. Will it be beneficial overall?

   (ii) Compare the benefits and disadvantages of two major infrastructure projects in very different countries.

   (iii) Is it more important to renew ageing infrastructure or to develop new infrastructure?

   (iv) Your own research question.

(b) Choose one of these projects. Use skills development Activity 9 on page 95 to help you plan and carry out your project.

   (i) Produce a video campaign against a specific infrastructure project.

   (ii) How could the infrastructure in your school be improved? Put together a proposal to persuade your head teacher to make some changes.

   (iii) Design your own country/city/school with basic infrastructure. You could use a computer game of paper for your design. Justify your choices and present your design to an audience.

   (iv) A project of your choice.

Activity 9.1

Think about which research questions or project outcome you would like to try from the list of suggestions. You can use the next few activities to help you research, think and decide.

If you are choosing your own project, remember to set a SMART outcome (see page 14).

If you are entering your project for examination, you must include cross-cultural collaboration.

Activity 9.2

What types of infrastructure and transport does each of these individuals need?

(a) A subsistence farmer in Kenya

(b) A Kenyan flower farmer selling to a European market

(c) An American tourist on holiday in Kenya

(d) A student in a school

(e) A teacher in a school

Think about the different perspectives these people have. What are the needs, expectations, beliefs, and desires that make their perspectives different?

Figure 9.1 Are there skateboard lockers in your school?

Planning a line of inquiry

You need to plan your line of inquiry. Look back at the Section 3 skills development activities on pages 87–88 to remind yourself of the stages of planning an inquiry.

Activity 9.3

- Think about your search terms and change them if you don't get results

- Skim read for key words and phrases before you read in detail.

- Keep notes on key ideas – you will need them later

- Keep a list of references so you can find information again

(a) What are the most important transport and infrastructure problems in your area?

    (i) What do you already think? Are you prepared to change your mind?

    (ii) What search terms will you use?

    (iii) What key words and phrases will you skim read for?

    (iv) Remember to think about which problems are most important, and why.

(b) Choose a city or country in a very different part of the world. What are their most important transport and infrastructure problems?

(c) What are the similarities and differences in the transport and infrastructure problems experienced by these two areas?

(d) Add your own questions to help you plan your own line of inquiry to answer your own question. Use diagrams to help you.

Question

When you are questioning the ideas, information and perspectives that you have found during your research, you can ask:

- Do I need to cross-check the facts?

- Are any predicted consequences likely and realistic?

Remember

Remember also to ask the questions you practised in Sections 1 and 2 as well.

Activity 9.4

Go through materials you have found in your research.

(a) Cross-check the facts that you want to use.

(b) Is this a good quality source?

(c) Is the reasoning good, or are there problems that mean I shouldn't believe it?

(d) What other questions do you need to ask?

Cross-checking facts

Activity 9.5

Figure 9.2 The Shanghai skyline is sometimes obscured by fog

Document 1

XueFei: 'In Shanghai, where I work, the infrastructure is new and growing fast. But the pace of change is too fast, and the pollution is often so bad you can hardly breathe or see. This is going to get worse. By contrast, in my home village, my parents don't have running water or electricity.'

Mark: 'Here in the UK our infrastructure is getting old. It can't cope with the demands of modern life. Some of our sewers are over 150 years old and our trains are twentieth century. We need a new airport to keep business growing, but people oppose this because it might damage the environment.'

Alina: 'I want to sell the jewellery I make online. But our internet connection is so unreliable, and the postal service is terrible. Half the things I post go to the postman's mother/wife/daughter and never get to my customers. We need to invest a lot of money in this country's infrastructure. But who's going to pay for it?

(a) Find and write down one fact, one opinion and one prediction in what XueFei says.

(b) XueFei says, "the pollution is so bad you can hardly breathe or see." Do you think this is a fact or an exaggeration?

(c) How would you check what the pollution is like in Shanghai? See if you can find out.

(d) Mark says that infrastructure in the UK "can't cope with the demands of modern life." Is this a fact or an opinion? Why do you think this?

(e) How would you find out more about whether UK infrastructure can cope with modern life? See how much information you can find in ten minutes.

(f) Do you think business or the environment is more important? Why?

(g) "Half the things I post go to the postman's mother/wife/daughter and never get to my customers." How far do you think this is a fact and how far an opinion? Why?

(h) How would you check this claim to see if it is a fact?

(i) Do you think Alina lives in a high, medium or low economic development country? Why? Does everyone in the class agree?

> **Remember**
>
> Remember, facts can be verified and opinions cannot.

> Think about your search terms. If "UK infrastructure modern life" doesn't work, what other search terms could you try?

Consequences

Activity 9.6

(a) Look at your research materials again and think about whether any predicted consequences are likely and realistic.

- Are the predicted consequences exaggerated?
- Are the consequences oversimplified?
- Are there other possibilities which are ignored?

(b) What are you going to do if your research materials predict unlikely consequences?

Activity 9.7

Copy and complete the table, using your own infrastructure ideas as well as the suggestions.

(a) Think about consequences for:

- different groups of people
- business
- the environment

(b) Think about the consequences of the consequences.

Infrastructure	Consequences of not having it	Consequences of getting it
Irrigation for a flower farm	Flowers won't grow in arid parts of Kenya. The flower farmer won't be able to develop the business.	Water used for the flower farm won't be available for other farmers (and so...). People will work at the flower farm instead of on their own land.
Airports		
Hotels with electricity, swimming pools, etc.		

Realistic and likely consequences

Infrastructure may be necessary for modern life – but how much is enough? Remember to think about possible negative consequences of infrastructure development, like damage to the environment or money wasted on pointless projects.

Activity 9.8

(a) How likely are these consequences? Discuss and explain your answers.

If the Kenyan farmer irrigates his flower farm…

If the Kenyan flower farmer irrigates his flower farm…	1	2	3
His flower-selling business will definitely be a success.			
All the other farmers in Kenya will starve to death.			
There will be some conflicts about water usage.			
He will have a good chance of making his business work.			
His flowers will grow.			

Remember to think about exaggeration, oversimplification and ignoring other possibilities.

Use the numbering as follows:

1. Serious exaggeration/highly unlikely
2. Quite likely
3. Very likely

(b) Work in groups to create activities like this for your classmates.

Bringing your skills together

Activity 9.9

A malicious software worm called Stuxnet has infected computer systems that control power plants, water treatment facilities and airports. In 2010 Iran's nuclear project was infected with this worm. In 2012 a US power plant was closed down for three weeks by the Stuxnet software worm, brought in accidentally by a contractor on a USB stick. The US Department of Homeland Security said that in 2012 energy companies, public water facilities and other infrastructure facilities reported 198 cyber incidents.

A: "This is the new terrorism and it's going to unleash a new era of dysfunction, disaster and disease on our planet! They're going to turn our own facilities against us – nuclear power plants will explode! We'll get radiation sickness! We'll have no electricity! Our water will bring typhoid and death into our homes!!"

B: "It's all a conspiracy."

C: "This is a very serious risk but I think we should trust our figures of authority to sort it out. They're the government so they must be in control."

(a) Is the US Department of Homeland Security a good source of information on Stuxnet infections in the US?

(b) Do you think A's reasoning is good? Why (not)?

(c) Is it all a conspiracy? Justify your answer.

(d) How far do you agree with C? Refer to the reasoning and use your own opinions.

Reflect and plan

Activity 9.10

(a) Have you changed your opinions about infrastructure generally?

(b) Is there a particular infrastructure debate in your local area? Do you see the issues differently now? If so, how? Why?

(c) Use diagrams and mind map to help you reflect on the issue for your research report.

Activity 9.11

(a) What is the best action to take in the case of the Kenyan flower farmer? Why is it best? How will you take all the different perspectives into consideration?

(b) What is the best action to take to deal with the malicious software worm Stuxnet? Why is it best? How will you take all the different perspectives into consideration?

Activity 9.12

Use the project planning process guidance on pages 95–98 of the skills development activities for Section 3 to help you to plan your project.

Present your findings and act on them

Activity 9.13

Produce a research report, using pages 98–104 of the skills development activities for Section 3. You should:

- Produce a short spoken presentation or video.
- Use diagrams, photos and other visual material.
- Write 750 words

> Work with a school from another country or a different cultural community in your own country.

Activity 9.14

Carry out your project.

After you have carried out your project, answer these questions:

(a) How well did the cross-cultural collaboration work this time?

(b) How well did your team work together?

(c) What problems did you have? How did you solve these problems?

(d) How will you avoid these problems next time?

> ### Remember
> Remember to review and amend your plan if you need to.

> Check with your teacher to make sure that you have completed the correct documents if you want to submit your project for assessment.

Section 3
10 Urbanization

In Sections 1 and 2 you practised producing individual research reports and group projects. Now you will be producing a full-length work that you could submit for assessment. You will also be doing activities that will enable you to practise the skills you need and help you prepare for the kinds of question that you may find in the written paper.

What is urbanization?

Research information

Suggested research questions and project outcomes

(a) Choose one of these research questions.

   (i)   How effectively is my country meeting the challenges of rapid urbanization? What else should the government do?

   (ii) How can we ensure that rapid urbanization does not lead to an increase in urban poverty?

   (iii) In developed countries, some old cities are shrinking. What is the best way to deal with the challenges that this brings?

   (iv) Your own research question.

(b) Choose one of these projects. Use skills development Activity 9 on page 95 to help you plan and carry out your project.

   (i)   Produce a video campaign to raise awareness of a problem associated with rapid urbanization.

   (ii) What actions need to be taken to improve the urban environment in a city of your choice? Put together a proposal to persuade the city leaders to take action.

   (iii) Using computer software or a pencil and paper, design your own new city. Justify your choices and present your design to an audience.

   (iv) A project of your choice.

If you do decide to submit work from this section for assessment, come back and check it again after you have worked through Sections 4 and 5.

If you are setting your own research question, make sure that the question allows you to look at causes, consequences, personal, national and global perspectives, and possible solutions.

If you are choosing your own project, remember to set a SMART outcome (see page 14).

Activity 10.1

Think about which research questions or project outcome you would like to try from the list of suggestions. You can use the next few activities to help you research, think and decide.

Remember

If you are entering your project for assessment, you must include cross-cultural collaboration.

Activity 10.2

(a) What are the challenges and benefits of rapid urbanization for each of these individuals?

  (i) A labourer who has migrated to the city to find work

  (ii) A school student

  (iii) The owner of a new computer business

  (iv) A commuter

  (v) A city leader

(b) Think about the different perspectives that these people have. What are the needs, expectations, beliefs and desires that make their perspectives different?

(c) To what extent is urbanization a personal, national or global concern?

Planning a line of inquiry

You need to plan your line of inquiry. Look back at the Section 3 skills development activities on pages 87–88, to remind yourself of the stages of planning an inquiry.

- Think about your search terms and change them if you don't get results.

- Skim-read for key words and phrases before you read in detail.

- Keep notes on key ideas – you will need them later.

- Keep a list of references so that you can find information again.

Activity 10.3

(a) What are the most important problems in your area related to urbanization?

  (i) What do you already think? Are you prepared to change your mind?

  (ii) What search terms will you use?

  (iii) What key words and phrases will you skim-read for?

  (iv) Remember to think about which problems are most important, and why.

(b) Choose a city or country in another, very different part of the world. What are its most important problems related to urbanization?

(c) What are the similarities and differences in the urbanization problems experienced by these two areas?

(d) Add your own questions to help you plan your line of inquiry to answer your research question. Use diagrams to help you.

Question

When you are questioning the ideas, information, and perspectives that you have found during your research, you can ask:

- Do I need to cross-check the facts?

- How likely and realistic are the predicted consequences?

> **Remember**
>
> Ask the questions you practised in Sections 1 and 2 as well.

Activity 10.4

Go through the materials you have found in your research.

(a) Cross-check the facts you want to use.

(b) Ask yourself how good-quality this source is.

(c) How good is the reasoning? Are any problems bad enough that you shouldn't believe it?

(d) What other questions do you need to ask?

Cross-checking facts

Activity 10.5

> **Javier:** "We have to take action to prevent so many people from moving into cities. Urbanization is causing terrible overcrowding in slums, insanitary conditions, and illness, and it's putting unmanageable pressure on cities' resources."
>
> **Ngoc:** "We can't prevent urbanization. It's happening, so we have to deal with it. If governments and city leaders make good decisions, urbanization will be a good thing. For example, my city, Hanoi, has grown, but we don't have large slums, because the government made strict rules about land use."
>
> **Kefilwe:** "If you look at world statistics, the more urbanized nations have higher life expectancy and literacy rates. Innovation thrives in cities, and 80 per cent of world gross domestic product (GDP) is generated in cities. So Ngoc is right. But here in South Africa, the government decided to build two million homes on cheap land outside cities – and didn't provide transport links. So it takes three hours to get to work."

(a) Javier says, "We have to take action to prevent so many people from moving into cities." Is this a fact or an opinion? Explain your answer.

(b) "It's putting unmanageable pressure on cities' resources." Is this a fact or an exaggeration? Explain your answer.

(c) How would you check what effects urbanization is having on your city/local area? See how much information you can find in ten minutes.

(d) Identify and write down one opinion and one prediction that Ngoc makes.

(e) How would you check whether Hanoi really has grown without forming large slums? See how much information you can find in ten minutes.

(f) "More urbanized nations have higher life expectancy and literacy rates." How would you check this claim to see if it is a fact?

(g) "Ngoc is right." Is this a fact or an opinion? Explain your answer.

(h) "It takes three hours to get to work." Is this a fact or an exaggeration? How would you check?

> **Remember**
>
> Facts can be verified but opinions cannot.

> Think about your search terms. If your first search doesn't work, what other search terms could you try?

Consequences

(a) Look at your research materials again and think about likely and realistic any predicted consequences are.

- Are the predicted consequences exaggerated?
- Are the consequences oversimplified?
- Are there other possibilities that are ignored?

(b) What are you going to do if your research materials predict unlikely consequences?

Activity 10.7

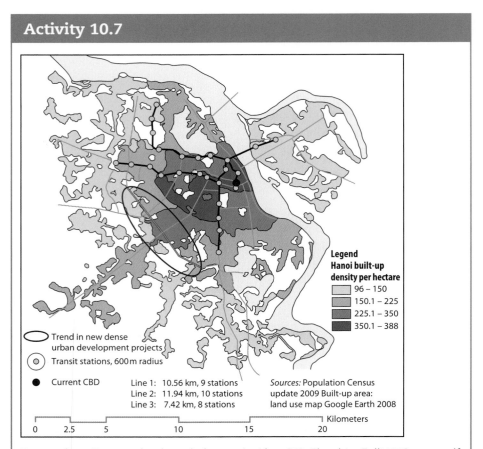

Legend
Hanoi built-up density per hectare

- 96 – 150
- 150.1 – 225
- 225.1 – 350
- 350.1 – 388

Trend in new dense urban development projects

Transit stations, 600 m radius

Current CBD

Line 1: 10.56 km, 9 stations
Line 2: 11.94 km, 10 stations
Line 3: 7.42 km, 8 stations

Sources: Population Census update 2009 Built-up area: land use map Google Earth 2008

Kilometers
0   2.5   5   10   15   20

Source: http://www.urbanknowledge.org/ur/docs/UR_Flagship_Full%20Report.pdf

Figure 10.1 Urban development and rail links in Hanoi

(a) Look at the image of Hanoi. What are the likely consequences of dense urban development projects (such as businesses and homes) in an area that is not served by the new train system?

(b) In some cities, central slums are being cleared. What are the likely consequences for slum dwellers, other residents, local businesses, and commuters?

> **Remember**
>
> Think about exaggeration, oversimplification, and ignoring other possibilities.

Realistic and likely consequences

Activity 10.8

(a) How likely are the following consequences? Discuss and explain your answers.

    (i) If the government provides cheap but unreliable electricity to everyone…

    (ii) If the government provides reliable electricity to businesses…

Consequence	1	2	3
…the economy will grow			
…people will work from home instead of migrating to the city			
…there will be problems financing the electricity long term			
…there will be frequent power cuts			
…quality of life will be dramatically improved			

    (1) Serious exaggeration/highly unlikely

    (2) Quite likely

    (3) Very likely

(b) Work in groups to create activities like this for your classmates.

Bringing your skills together

Activity 10.9

One method of price discrimination is to offer the poor a specially tailored price quality mix. For example, poor people who can afford to buy water at times – but not regularly – can do so by the bucket. Or the poor can be served by simpler pipelines. In other ways, too, the poor can be offered flexible service that is better than what they had before, yet not exactly what the rich receive. (Water that is not fully treated can still serve many common uses, such as flushing toilets. Poor people can make their water potable by boiling it.)

Source: http://www.urbanknowledge.org/ur/docs/UR_Flagship_Full%20Report.pdf

A: "This is just another instance of discrimination against poor people and treating them like they're not fully human. If we can't provide proper services for everyone in society, we have no hope of achieving a society in which every child has the opportunity to succeed."

B: "Some clean water is clearly better than no clean water. But what worries me is that poor people – especially those who are desperate and/or poorly educated – will end up drinking the not fully treated water and becoming ill, which will make it harder for them to earn money, and could put pressure on health care systems (if they exist)."

C: "Nobody should have to buy water. It's OK to have luxuries available to the rich but not the poor, but clean water is not a luxury."

(a) Is http://www.urbanknowledge.org/ur/ docs/UR_Flagship_Full%20Report.pdf a good source of information and expert opinions on issues relating to urbanization? Explain your answer.

(b) How good do you think A's reasoning is?

(c) How likely are the consequences that B predicts?

(d) How far do you agree with C? Refer to the reasoning and use your own opinions.

Reflect and plan

Activity 10.10

(a) Have you changed your opinions about urbanization generally? If so, in what way? If not, why not?

(b) Is there a particular urbanization debate in your local area? Do you see the issues differently now? If so, how and why?

(c) Use diagrams and mind maps to help you reflect on the issue for your research report.

What is the best action to take?

Activity 10.11

(a) What is the best action to take in the provision of electricity? Why and how?

(b) What is the best action to take to ensure that everyone has at least some access to water? Why and how?

Activity 10.12

Use the guidance on project planning (pages 95–98) in the skills development activities for this section to help you plan your project.

> Work with a school from another country or a different cultural community in your own country.

Present your findings and act on them

Activity 10.13

Produce a research report, using the guidance in the skills development activities for Section 3 (on pages 98–104). You should:

- produce a short spoken presentation or video
- use diagrams, photos and other visual material
- write 750 words.

> **Remember**
>
> You can always review and amend your plan if you need to.

Activity 10.14

Carry out your group project. Then answer these questions:

(a) How well did the cross-cultural collaboration work this time?

(b) How well did your team work together?

(c) What problems did you have?

(d) How did you solve these problems?

(e) How will you avoid these problems next time?

> Check with your teacher that you have completed the correct documents if you want to submit your project for assessment.

Section 3
11 Disease and health

In Sections 1 and 2 you practised producing individual research reports and group projects. Now you will be producing a full-length work that you could submit for assessment. You will also be doing activities that will enable you to practise the skills you need and help you prepare for the kinds of question that you may find in the written paper.

Research information

> If you do decide to submit work from this section for assessment, come back and check it again after you have worked through Sections 4 and 5.

Suggested research questions and project outcomes

(a) Choose one of these research questions.

   (i) How effectively is my country dealing with health issues? What else should the government do?

   (ii) How can we break the cycle of disease and poverty?

   (iii) Should governments put more emphasis on maintaining good health rather than curing disease?

   (iv) Your own research question.

(b) Choose one of these projects. Use skills development Activity 9 on page 95 to help you plan and carry out your project.

   (i) Produce a video campaign to raise awareness of health issues for students in two different countries.

   (ii) What actions need to be taken to improve healthcare in a country of your choice? Put together a proposal to persuade the city leaders to take action.

   (iii) Using computer software or a pencil and paper, design your own healthcare system. Justify your choices and present your design to an audience.

   (iv) A project of your choice.

> If you are setting your own research question, make sure that the question allows you to look at causes, consequences, personal, national and global perspectives, and possible solutions.

> If you are choosing your own project, remember to set a SMART outcome (see page 14).

Remember

If you are entering your project for assessment, you must include cross-cultural collaboration.

Activity 11.1

Think about which research questions or project outcome you would like to try from the list of suggestions. You can use the next few activities to help you research, think and decide.

Activity 11.2

(a) What are the health issues most likely to affect the following individuals? Think about the differences in terms of the stage of economic development of the different countries.

    (i) A labourer who has migrated to Hanoi to find work

    (ii) A school student in Beijing

    (iii) A pregnant woman in Kampala

    (iv) A toddler in Glasgow

    (v) A business leader in Washington DC

(b) Think about the different perspectives that these people have. What are the needs, expectations, beliefs and desires that make their perspectives different?

(c) To what extent are disease and health personal, national or global concerns?

Planning a line of inquiry

You need to plan your line of inquiry. Look back at the Section 3 skills development activities on pages 87–88, to remind yourself of the stages of planning an inquiry.

- Think about your search terms and change them if you don't get results.
- Skim-read for key words and phrases before you read in detail.
- Keep notes on key ideas – you will need them later.
- Keep a list of references so that you can find information again.

Activity 11.3

(a) What are the most important problems in your area related to disease and health?

    (i) What do you already think? Are you prepared to change your mind?

    (ii) What search terms will you use?

    (iii) What key words and phrases will you skim-read for?

    (iv) Remember to think about which problems are most important, and why.

(b) Choose a city or country in another, very different part of the world. What are its most important problems related to disease and health?

(c) What are the similarities and differences in the health problems experienced by these two areas?

(d) Add your own questions to help you plan your line of inquiry to answer your research question. Use diagrams to help you.

Question

When you are questioning the ideas, information, and perspectives that you have found during your research, you can ask:

- Do I need to cross-check the facts?
- How realistic are any predicted consequences?

Remember

Ask the questions you practised in Sections 1 and 2 as well.

Activity 11.4

Go through the material you have found in your research.

(a) Cross-check the facts you want to use.

(b) Ask yourself how good-quality this source is.

(c) How good is the reasoning? Are any problems so bad that you shouldn't believe it?

(d) What other questions do you need to ask?

Cross-check facts

Activity 11.5

Antonia: "Around 75 per cent of deaths among people aged 10–24 in the US are caused by unintentional injuries or violence. More than half of child deaths in developing countries in 2001 were caused by acute respiratory infections, measles, diarrhoea, malaria, and HIV/AIDS. Added to this, in 2001 99 per cent of child deaths were in developing countries. It doesn't really matter if these young people are dying from preventable accidents or preventable diseases – it's just wrong."

Julian: "Here in Australia the major causes of ill health include heart disease and strokes, and these are caused mainly by poor lifestyle – bad diets, smoking and not enough exercise. It almost makes you wonder whether it's worth curing all the real diseases."

Qing Yu: "We've been having a debate in the UK about cigarette packaging. The evidence shows that young people are less likely to smoke if cigarettes come in plain packets. But the government has decided not to pass a law enforcing plain packets. Interestingly, one of the Prime Minister's advisers also works for two major cigarette firms. We don't have corruption in Britain – just 'hidden persuasion'."

(a) Identify two facts and an opinion given by Antonia. Explain your answer.

(b) Antonia compares statistics for 10–24-year-olds and children. How acceptable is this? Explain your answer.

(c) Can you check Antonia's facts? Can you find more recent figures?

(d) Julian says, "Here in Australia the major causes of ill health include heart disease and strokes, and these are caused mainly by poor lifestyle – bad diets, smoking and not enough exercise." Is this a fact or an opinion? Explain your answer.

> **Remember**
>
> Facts can be verified but opinions cannot.

(e) "It almost makes you wonder whether it's worth curing all the real diseases." Do you agree? Why (not)?

(f) "Young people are less likely to smoke if cigarettes come in plain packets." How would you check this claim to see whether it is a fact?

(g) "We don't have corruption in Britain – just 'hidden persuasion'." Is this a fact or an opinion? Explain your answer.

> Think about your search terms. If your first search doesn't work, what other search terms could you try?

Consequences

Activity 11.6

(a) Look at your research materials again and think about how likely and realistic any predicted consequences are.

- Are the predicted consequences exaggerated?

- Are the consequences oversimplified?
- Are there other possibilities that are ignored?

(b) What are you going to do if your research materials predict unlikely consequences?

Activity 11.7

(a) What are the likely consequences of allowing people to choose their lifestyle freely, with no government intervention?

(b) What are the likely consequences of the government trying to change people's lifestyle choices? Does it vary depending on which country you think about?

> **Remember**
>
> Think about exaggeration, oversimplification, and ignoring other possibilities.

Realistic and likely consequences

Activity 11.8

(a) How likely are the following consequences? Discuss and explain your answers.

If every woman gets free health care while she is pregnant...	1	2	3
...infant mortality rates will decrease			
...women will get pregnant just to get free health care			
...women will be educated about basic health and hygiene while pregnant			
...the health-care system will break down			
...women will have fewer children due to good medical advice			

    (1) Serious exaggeration/highly unlikely

    (2) Quite likely

    (3) Very likely

(b) Work in groups to create activities like this for your classmates.

Bringing your skills together

Activity 11.9

Should health care be free?

A: "Health care is a basic human right, and should therefore be free to all citizens. No one should have to choose between food and medication, or heat and going to the doctor. In addition, no one should face bankruptcy because of an illness or accident. Everyone should have access to health care."

B: "Free health care, yes, and so if you are for free health care, you are for abortion. If you want to add more taxes to the ballot, paying for your health care, firemen, law enforcement services, and so much more, let's do it! You all think you do not pay for other services, but you do; however, this service will make the economy more depressed than it is now, adding more fees by governments to the employer and so forth. *Huge* companies need to pay for health care, especially when their CEOs make $5 million plus a year – *they* need to pay for health care..."

C: "No, health care should not be free. Nothing in life is 'free.' Health-care services that a person doesn't pay for might seem 'free' to that person, but someone else is paying for them. Any good or service that a person receives should be paid for, and the person should know how much it costs. People are completely out of touch with the true and exorbitant cost of health care. It's like we're demanding the government provides us with free diamonds."

D: "I don't want the government deciding whether I get to live or die. And that's what free health care means. Also, why should idiots who contribute to their own illness and injury get free health care? Don't smoke, don't go skiing, don't drive like a maniac. Simple."

Follow   **Discuss**

(a) How reliable are these sources? Justify your answer.

(b) How likely are the consequences that B predicts? In other respects, how good is the reasoning? Explain your answers.

(c) How good do you think C's reasoning is? Why?

(d) Whose view do you most agree with? Refer to the reasoning and use your own opinions.

Reflect and plan

Activity 11.10

(a) Have you changed your opinions about disease and health issues generally? If so, in what way? If not, why not?

(b) Is there a particular health debate in your local area? Do you see the issues differently now? If so, how and why?

(c) Use diagrams and mind maps to help you reflect on the issue for your research report.

What is the best action to take?

Activity 11.11

(a) What is the best action to take to ensure that people make healthy lifestyle choices?

(b) What is the best action to take to ensure that everyone has at least some access to healthcare?

Activity 11.12

Use the guidance on project planning (pages 95–98) in the skills development activities for this section to help you plan your project.

> Work with a school from another country or a different cultural community in your own country.

Present your findings and take action

Activity 11.13

Produce a research report, using the guidance in the skills development activities for this section (pages 98–104). You should:

- produce a short spoken presentation or video
- use diagrams, photos, and other visual material
- write 750 words.

> ### Remember
>
> You can always review and amend your plan if you need to.

Activity 11.14

Carry out your group project. Then answer these questions:

(a) How well did the cross-collaboration work this time?

(b) How well did your team work together?

(c) What problems did you have?

(d) How did you solve these problems?

(e) How will you avoid these problems next time?

> Check with your teacher that you have completed the correct documents if you want to submit your project for assessment.

Section 3
12 Poverty and inequality

In Sections 1 and 2 you practised producing individual research reports and group projects. Now you will be producing a full-length work that you could submit for assessment. You will also be doing activities that will enable you to practise the skills you need and help you prepare for the kinds of question that you may find in the written paper.

Research information

If you do decide to submit work from this section for assessment, come back and check it again after you have worked through Sections 4 and 5.

Suggested research questions and project outcomes

(a) Choose one of these research questions.

(i) How effectively is my country meeting the challenges of inequality – in income, consumption, and treatment? What else should the government do?

(ii) Is a minimum level of income a matter of justice?

(iii) Do we help poor people more by providing aid or by trading with them?

(iv) Your own research question.

(b) Choose one of these projects. Use skills development Activity 9 on page 95 to help you plan and carry out your project.

(i) Produce a video campaign to raise awareness of a problem associated with poverty or inequality.

(ii) What actions need to be taken to reduce poverty and inequality in a city of your choice? Put together a proposal to persuade the city leaders to take action.

(iii) A project of your choice.

If you are setting your own research question, make sure that the question allows you to look at causes, consequences, personal, national and global perspectives, and possible solutions.

If you are choosing your own project, remember to set a SMART outcome (see page 14).

Remember

If you are entering your project for assessment, you must include cross-cultural collaboration.

Activity 12.1

Think about which research questions or project outcome you would like to try from the list of suggestions. You can use the next few activities to help you research, think and decide.

Activity 12.2

(a) What are the problems associated with poverty and inequality for the following people?

    (i)   A labourer who has migrated to the city to find work

    (ii) A school student from a disadvantaged background

    (iii) A young migrant mother with two children and asthma

    (iv) A builder with a bad back

    (v)   A salesperson whose employer has shut down and who lives in a declining town near their elderly mother.

(b) Think about the different perspectives that these people have. What are the needs, expectations, beliefs and desires that make their perspectives different?

(c) To what extent are poverty and inequality personal, national or global concerns?

Planning a line of inquiry

You need to plan your line of inquiry. Look back at the Section 3 skills development activities on pages 87–88, to remind yourself of the stages of planning an inquiry.

- Think about your search terms and change them if you don't get results.
- Skim-read for key words and phrases before you read in detail.
- Keep notes on key ideas – you will need them later.
- Keep a list of references so that you can find information again.

Activity 12.3

(a) What are the most important problems in your area related to poverty and inequality?

    (i)   What do you already think? Are you prepared to change your mind?

    (ii) What search terms will you use?

    (iii) What key words and phrases will you skim-read for?

    (iv) Remember to think about which problems are most important, and why.

(b) Choose a city or country in another, very different part of the world. What are its most important problems related to poverty and inequality?

(c) What are the similarities and differences in the poverty and inequality problems experienced by these two areas?

(d) Add your own questions to help you plan your line of inquiry to answer your research question. Use diagrams to help you.

Question

When you are questioning the ideas, information, and perspectives that you have found during your research, you can ask:

- Do I need to cross-check the facts?

- How realistic are any predicted consequences?

Remember

Ask the questions you practised in Sections 1 and 2 as well.

Activity 12.4

Go through the material you have found in your research.

(a) Cross-check the facts you want to use.

(b) Ask yourself how good-quality this source is.

(c) How good is the reasoning? Are any problems so bad that you shouldn't believe it?

(d) What other questions do you need to ask?

Cross-checking facts

Activity 12.5

A well-known restaurant has partnered with Visa to make a website dedicated to showing its employees how to properly budget their meagre peasant salaries. However, what it actually does is illustrate the fact that it is nearly impossible to get by on minimum wage, as shown in this "example" budget chart:

That is actually what you would make if you were working *full time* at the restaurant: 1,105 dollars a month.

Now let's say that the "second" job that they budget in here is also minimum wage. The national minimum wage is $7.25. That translates to *74 hours* a week. That's almost a whole other full-time job.

And what do you get for working 74 hours a week? Well, you don't get heat, clearly. Also noticeably absent in this budget? Food. And gas. There is really no such thing as health insurance for $20 a month.

Right now, we have people in our government saying that we shouldn't even have a minimum wage. That employers should be free to pay people whatever they can get someone to agree to work for. If they can get someone to work for $3 an hour, then it should be allowed.

There are people who comfort themselves by telling themselves that poor people are only poor because poor people are *lazy*. Pretty sure someone who works 74 hours a week isn't lazy.

You may think that most of these minimum wage earners are teenagers. Well, 87.9 per cent of minimum wage earners are over the age of 20, and 28 per cent of those people are parents trying to raise a kid on this budget. That is not a good thing for our future and it is not a good thing for our economy. In order for the economy to thrive, people have to be able to buy things.

Source: Adapted from: http://www.deathandtaxesmag.com/202172/

Sample Monthly Budget	
Monthly Net Income	
Income (1st Job)	$ 1,105
Income (2nd Job)	$ 955
Other Income	$ 0
Monthly Net Income Total	$ 2,060
Monthly Expenses	
Savings	$ 100
Mortgage/Rent	$ 600
Car Payment	$ 150
Car/Home Insurance	$ 100
Health Insurance	$ 20
Heating	$ 0
Cable/Phone	$ 100
Electric	$ 90
Other	$ 100
Monthly Expenses Total	$ 1,260
Monthly Spending Total	$ 800
(*Monthly Net Income Total minus Monthly Expenses Total*)	
Daily Spending Money Goal	$ 27
(*Monthly Spending Money divided by 30*)*	
*the average of 30 days in a month is used to simplify your budget	

(a) "The national minimum wage is $7.25 [in the US in 2013]." What is the national minimum wage there now?

(b) What is the national minimum wage in your country, or in another country?

(c) "There really is no such thing as health insurance for $20 a month." Is this a fact or an opinion? Explain your answer.

(d) How would you check what health insurance in the US costs?

(e) "Someone who works 74 hours a week isn't lazy." Is this a fact or an opinion? Explain your answer.

(f) "87.9 per cent of minimum wage earners [in the US] are over the age of 20." Can you cross-check this fact? Is the figure the same now as in 2013, when the article was written?

(g) "If they can get someone to work for $3 an hour, then it should be allowed." Is this an opinion or a prediction? Justify your answer.

> **Remember**
>
> Facts can be verified but opinions cannot.

> Think about your search terms. If your first search doesn't work, what other search terms could you try?

Consequences

Activity 12.6

(a) Look at your research materials again and think about how likely and realistic any predicted consequences are.

- Are the predicted consequences exaggerated?
- Are the consequences oversimplified?
- Are there other possibilities that are ignored?

(b) What are you going to do if your research materials predict unlikely consequences?

Activity 12.7

(a) What are the likely consequences for the children of parents who earn the minimum wage?

(b) What are the likely consequences for businesses if the minimum wage is significantly raised?

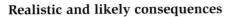

Realistic and likely consequences

Activity 12.8

(a) How likely are the following consequences? Discuss and explain your answers.

If a maximum wage is introduced...	1	2	3
...rich people will leave the country			
...there will be less envy-based crime			
...everyone would be much happier			
...there would be no reason to work hard			
...rich people would find other ways to stay rich			

    (1) Serious exaggeration/highly unlikely

    (2) Quite likely

    (3) Very likely

(b) Work in groups to create activities like this for your classmates.

> **Remember**
>
> Think about exaggeration, oversimplification, and ignoring other possibilities.

Bringing your skills together

Activity 12.9

A: "There are people out there earning less than $1 a day, and we are arguing about $7.25 an hour? These people live in the richest nation in the world. They should get their act together."

B: "We should get rid of the minimum wage as it has been one of our country's main causes of unemployment. Just like prices, wages need to be set by the market. The main earners of the minimum wage were minorities and teenagers. Increasing the minimum wage meant that companies got rid of these employees and left a growing percentage of the population without the basic skills they needed for higher-level jobs.

The minimum wage was raised significantly in 2007, and this led to a widespread loss of employment and the recession. We should abolish the minimum wage in order to help the young and the poor."

C: "Can you show me written evidence for any of these entirely inaccurate statements?"

D: "Minimum wage increases are good for business. You need to pay your employees enough to buy the products you make. If people have more money, they'll spend more – in local shops and restaurants, for instance – and you can raise prices without too much opposition."

(a) How good are these comments as a source of information or expert opinion on issues relating to the minimum wage?

(b) How likely are the causes and consequences that B suggests?

(c) How good do you think D's reasoning is?

(d) Whose view are you most in agreement with? Refer to the reasoning and use your own opinions.

Reflect and plan

Activity 12.10

(a) Have you changed your opinions about poverty and inequality generally?

(b) Is there a particular debate about poverty and inequality in your local area? Do you see the issues differently now? If so, why and in what way?

(c) Use diagrams and mind maps to help you reflect on the issue for your research report.

What is the best action to take?

Activity 12.11

(a) What is the best action to take to reduce poverty? Give reasons.

(b) What is the best action to take to reduce inequality? Give reasons.

Activity 12.12

Use the guidance on project planning (pages 95–98) in the skills development activities for this section to help you plan your project.

> Work with a school from another country or a different cultural community in your own country.

Present your findings and take action

Activity 12.13

Produce a research report, using the guidance in the skills development activities for this section (pages 98–104). You should:

- produce a short spoken presentation or video
- use diagrams, photos, and other visual material
- write 750 words.

> **Remember**
>
> You can always review and amend your plan if you need to.

Activity 12.14

Carry out your group project. Then answer these questions:

(a) How well did the cross-cultural collaboration work this time?

(b) How well did your team work together?

(c) What problems did you have?

(d) How did you solve these problems?

(e) How will you avoid these problems next time?

> Check with your teacher that you have completed the correct documents if you want to submit your project for assessment.

Section 4
Skills development activities

In this section you will be revising and practising the skills you developed in Sections 1 to 3, using these topic areas:

- Employment
- Technology and the economic divide
- Law and criminality
- Trade and aid.

You will now begin using your skills much more independently. You will also be extending your skills, particularly the evaluation and presentation of your reasoning. In addition to working towards a research report and group project, you will start to practise questions like those you'll be doing in the written exam. (The sample answers in this section have been written by the author. The way marks are awarded in the real assessment might be different).

Research information

You should now be fairly confident about researching information and planning a line of inquiry. Remember the main stages of your inquiry:

1. Ask plenty of questions (draw diagrams).

2. Use quick searches to gain ideas.

3. Think about key issues, perspectives, causes, and consequences (draw diagrams).

4. Think about possible solutions and further consequences.

5. Decide what interests you.

6. Set a question.

7. Find and select information to answer your question.

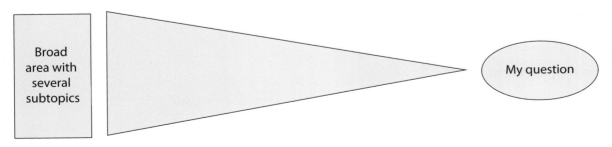

Figure 1 The initial stage narrowed down to a question

Work in groups, share your thinking, and bounce ideas off one another. Use quick Internet searches, and think about key issues, perspectives, and causes and consequences.

(a) Use the following questions to start your thinking on the topic of employment. Draw diagrams to help you, as you follow ideas or add more questions.

   (i) What difference does having a job make to an individual?

   (ii) What difference do unemployment rates make to communities or countries?

   (iii) Who is (or who should be) responsible for creating jobs? Is it governments, companies, or individuals?

   (iv) Is it right to define or judge people by their jobs?

   (v) Is it better to have local or multinational companies creating jobs? Are personal and national perspectives different?

(b) Use these questions to start your thinking about technology and the economic divide. Draw diagrams to help you, as you follow ideas or add more questions.

   (i) Which technology is the most important for economic development – communications technology like the Internet, military technology, medical technology, engineering technology, or something else?

   (ii) In what ways can broadband Internet access help improve a local economy?

   (iii) Can we change the way the world is divided into rich and poor? Should we? If so, how?

   (iv) Who should invest in technology – governments, international organizations like the UN, multinational companies, individuals, or someone else?

   (v) Should companies own technology or should everyone share the benefits?

(c) Write your own list of questions to start your thinking on law and criminality. Share these questions with another group. Use their questions to help you too. Draw diagrams to help you, as you follow ideas or add more questions.

(d) Write your own list of questions to start your thinking on trade and aid. Share these questions with another group. Use their questions to help you too. Draw diagrams to help you, as you follow ideas or add more questions.

Question setting

When you are preparing an individual research report, remember to set a question that will help you to:

- develop a line of reasoning (argument and explanation)
- consider a current problem or issue
- consider causes and consequences (positive and negative) of the problem or issue
- consider personal, national, and global perspectives
- think of possible solutions or courses of action

- consider the consequences (positive and negative) of these possible solutions
- decide on the best course of action
- answer within the word limit.

Activity 2

(a) Do you think any of the following are good questions to use for an individual research report? Give your reasons why or why not.

(i) How can we create more jobs in my region?

(ii) What were the causes of the economic crisis in 2008?

(iii) Should people in developed countries give their old computers to people in developing countries?

(iv) What is the best way to help struggling communities in my region/in developing countries?

(v) Should we punish criminals?

(vi) What are the best ways to deal with international crimes such as smuggling?

(vii) What are the benefits of trade and aid?

(viii) In times of economic recession, should governments reduce the amount of aid they give to foreign countries?

(ix) What sorts of aid are there?

(x) Should murder be punishable by death?

(b) Working in pairs, think of one question for each of the four topic areas:

(i) Employment

(ii) Technology and the economic divide

(iii) Law and criminality

(iv) Trade and aid.

(c) Work with another pair. Can you improve each other's questions? Can you modify your question to make it fit the requirements?

> In part **(c)**, you should aim to improve, not criticise. "How are you going to deal with personal, national and global perspectives?" is more helpful than: "Your question's rubbish. It doesn't deal with international perspectives."

Exam strategies

By now, you've had quite a lot of practice in identifying issues, causes, problems, perspectives, and solutions. The next stage is to think about how you will identify them when you are under time pressure during the written exam. Here are some strategies you can use:

- Read the questions first quickly, so that you can look for the information you need when you read the resource booklet.

- Make notes in the resource booklet while you are reading it.

- Think about personal, national and global perspectives while you are reading.

- Use different colours to indicate problems, causes, consequences, and solutions in the resource booklet.

- Think about what the question is asking you to do – is it asking you to identify a reason or cause, to explain, summarize, or think about what is most important? – and make sure you do it.

Activity 3

Read the three documents below, and then look at the sample answers to the exam-style questions that follow. In each case, decide which answer is best.

Document 1

According to Interpol[*], trafficking in human beings is a multi-billion-dollar form of international organized crime, constituting modern-day slavery. Victims are recruited and trafficked between countries and regions using deception or coercion. They are stripped of their autonomy, freedom of movement and choice, and face various forms of physical and mental abuse.

The main types of human trafficking include:

- trafficking for forced labour
- trafficking of organs.

Closely connected is the issue of people smuggling, in which smugglers are paid to help individuals enter a country illegally.

Source: http://www.interpol.int/Crime-areas/Trafficking-in-human-beings/Trafficking-in-human-beings

[*] Interpol is an international police organization with 190 member countries. Its role is to enable police in different countries to work together to make the world a safer place.

Document 2

Iran's Deputy Ambassador to the UN, Gholam-Hossein Dehqani, urged the international community to take action on human trafficking. Poverty, unemployment, discrimination, a lack of social and economic opportunities, and global financial crises are among the factors making individuals vulnerable to human trafficking, Dehqani said. He stressed the responsibility of wealthy nations.

Source: http://www.presstv.ir/detail/2013/05/15/303607/iran-urges-action-on-human-trafficking/

Document 3

> A migrant domestic worker recounted her friend's experience of trying to escape from a situation of forced labour: "She managed to escape through a window, from the family that treated her like a slave. She was terrified and had bruises on her body. Her passport was locked in the house. The policeman at the station asked her for her documents. She of course did not have them and wanted to tell him what had happened, but he insisted on her documents first and said he must know who she was.
>
> **Source:** www.antislavery.org

(a) Explain in your own words the difference between human trafficking and people smuggling.   [2 marks]

Answer 1: Trafficking in human beings is a multi-billion-dollar form of international organized crime, constituting modern-day slavery. People smuggling is when smugglers are paid to help individuals enter a country illegally.

Answer 2: Human trafficking is lying to people and promising them jobs, but selling them into slavery or to have their organs given to rich sick people. People smuggling is when criminals take money from people to help them migrate illegally.

Answer 3: Human trafficking is different from people smuggling because it involves deceiving people into migrating and then selling or abusing them, whereas people smuggling only involves helping people to migrate illegally. Both are crimes, but human trafficking seems to be more of a crime.

(b) (i) Give three factors that make people vulnerable to human trafficking.   [3 marks]

Answer 1: Poverty, unemployment, discrimination

Answer 2: The discrimination make vulnerable. Economic opportunities a factor for trafficking. Wealthy nations responsible human trafficking.

(ii) Explain why one of these factors might cause people to be more vulnerable to human trafficking.   [4 marks]

Answer 1: If you have no job, you cannot feed your family and you can feel bad about yourself. If you can't get work at home, you need to look in other places to find work. Perhaps you are so desperate that you will pay someone money to find you work in Europe or America. That someone could deceive you.

Answer 2: Unemployment can make people vulnerable to human trafficking because it makes them more likely to be taken to another country and stripped of their autonomy, freedom of movement and choice, and face various forms of physical and mental abuse. Unemployment is a very bad experience.

(c) To what extent is human trafficking a personal, national or global problem? [6 marks]

Answer 1: Human trafficking is a global problem because it involves people being moved between countries. Document 1 says that this is "a multi-billion dollar form of international organized crime". Document 2 shows Iran's Deputy Ambassador to the UN urging the international community to take action and stressing the responsibility of wealthy nations. Document 3 shows how this is an issue of migrant domestic workers who need passports. So that's global.

Answer 2: Human trafficking is a personal problem for individuals involved. For the girl in document 3, she is in a personal hell, where her employers bruise her and the police won't help her. It's a national problem for the host nations, because people are being abused in their territory, and they need to take action to help individuals and prevent crime gangs. It's a global problem because the causes are global – global financial crises affecting local jobs – and the solutions need to be global, such as global policing.

What else do I need to know?

You have already thought about filling the gaps in your knowledge when you are researching a topic. In the exam, you may be asked about gaps in your knowledge. These are likely to be small, focused pieces of information but they may be important if you need them to come to a conclusion or to make a decision.

It is important to think about how this information will help you come to a conclusion or to make a decision. Let's look at an example.

> You are a police constable on duty. A young woman, bruised, bleeding and very upset comes up to you in the street. She says she is a legal migrant cleaner and that her employer is beating her. She wants to press charges against her employer.
>
> What do you need to know to decide whether the employer is guilty? How will you find the information you need? How will this help you decide whether the employer is guilty?

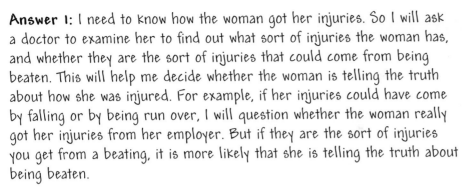

Do think about alternative possibilities. Don't jump to conclusions.

Answer 1: I need to know how the woman got her injuries. So I will ask a doctor to examine her to find out what sort of injuries the woman has, and whether they are the sort of injuries that could come from being beaten. This will help me decide whether the woman is telling the truth about how she was injured. For example, if her injuries could have come by falling or by being run over, I will question whether the woman really got her injuries from her employer. But if they are the sort of injuries you get from a beating, it is more likely that she is telling the truth about being beaten.

Comment: This is a very thorough answer, which focuses on the precise information needed, identifies a reliable way of getting the information, and explains how this will help to make a decision. It is clear that the information from the doctor will help to make a decision, but won't give certainty.

Answer 2: I need to know if the employer really beats his cleaner. I will ask a doctor to examine her. If the doctor says the injuries were made by a beating I will know that the woman is telling the truth and the employer is guilty. If the doctor says the injuries came from being run over, I will know that the cleaner is lying to get her employer into trouble.

Comment: This answer does identify an important piece of information that the police constable needs to know. Asking a doctor to examine the woman is a good way of getting useful evidence about the injuries. But in this answer, the comments about how the information will help are too extreme because, even if the doctor agrees that a beating could have caused the injuries, the woman's employer is not the only person who could have beaten her. So we cannot say, "I will know the woman is telling the truth" from this information. Also, if the woman's injuries came from being run over, we can *suspect* that the woman is lying, but she might be confused or mistaken (perhaps if she has been hit on the head) and we need much more information to be sure *why* she is lying.

Answer 3: I need to know whether the woman really is a cleaner. So I will ask her for details of her employer and interview the employer to find out what the woman does in her job. Then I will also ask the employer whether she beats her cleaner and why she does this.

Comment: This answer focuses on irrelevant information. It is not important to know whether this woman is a cleaner in order to decide whether her employer is guilty of beating her.

Activity 4

(a) You are the police constable in the scenario with the bruised, upset young woman.

   (i) Think of one question to ask the young woman to find out whether she really is a legal migrant. Explain how the answer might help.

   (ii) Think of one question to ask the woman's employer to find out whether she has employed a legal or illegal migrant as a cleaner. Explain how the answer might help.

   (iii) Think of one other person you could interview to help you find out what the situation is with the young woman and her employer. What question would you ask and how would it help?

(b) At 16.30 on Monday, a man with a scarf wrapped around his face walked into Treasure jewellery shop with a shotgun and stole diamond jewellery worth $20 000. Darius left work at the bank near Treasure at 16.20. He is seen on CCTV with a scarf wrapped around his face at 16.25. At 18.45 Darius met his girlfriend at a restaurant, and asked her to marry him. He gave her the ring she had spent many hours admiring in the window of Treasure. The police inspector decided that Darius must be the thief.

What do you need to know to decide whether Darius was the thief? How will this information help?

(c) The police in two countries are conducting some training to prevent human trafficking. They are concentrating on measures to:

   ● identify faked and forged passports

   ● check how hospitals get donor organs for transplants.

   (i) What do you need to know to decide whether this training is likely to be successful? How will this information help you decide?

   (ii) What other measures could the police include in their training? How would these measures help prevent human trafficking?

(d) Go back to your individual research report. Look for gaps in your knowledge. What else do you need to know? Think about how this knowledge will help you come to your conclusion or support a particular proposal for action.

Question

In Sections 1, 2 and 3 you considered a number of ways of questioning your information when you are doing individual research. They include asking four main types of question, as shown in this diagram.

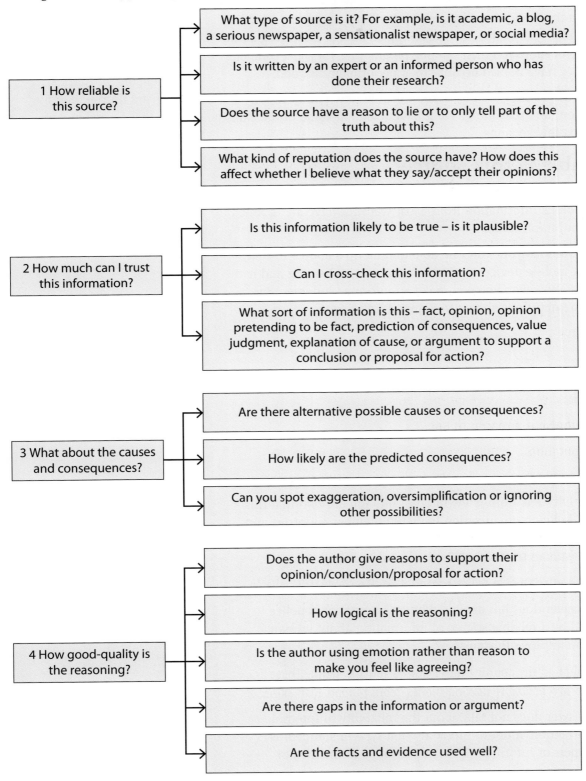

Figure 2 Questions to ask when researching

Figure 2 shows the questions you need to have in your mind all the time when you are researching, or even when you are just listening to the news or reading what people say on social media sites.

In your research report and in the project, you do not need to write down everything you have thought about every source. It will be obvious if you have thought about these questions, because you will use and quote reliable sources that make plausible claims. It's like seeing an athlete competing at the Olympics – they don't show you their training programme, they just compete. You can tell that they have trained because their performance is good.

In the written exam, you may well be asked to show how you question sources, information, and reasoning. We'll have a look at some of the skills involved in the next few sections.

You don't need to write these questions down in your research report in order to answer them.

Remember

If you decide that a source is unreliable, or that its claims are untrue, don't quote that source in your research report!

1 How reliable is this source?

When you are researching, you can look up a source to see how reliable it is, and where it took its information from. Most websites have an "About us" page with useful information.

In examination conditions you won't be able to look up a source to find out about it. Using mobile devices to find information is cheating and it is a serious offence. However, you can make an informed judgment by keeping in mind the questions shown in Figure 2, relating to:

- the type of source
- the author
- whether the author is using emotive or exaggerated language to get their point across
- whether the author has a reason to lie
- the author's reputation

Let's look at an example.

Document 1 in Activity 3 is from www.interpol.int. You are told that this is an international policing organization with 190 member countries and that it tries to make the world safer. How reliable is Interpol as a source of information about human trafficking? Explain your answer.

Answer 1: This is an international police organization. It's completely reliable.

Comment: This answer does not explain why an international police organization would be a reliable source of information about human trafficking. Can you improve this answer?

Answer 2: The police in my country don't always tell the truth. These international police are probably making money from human trafficking.

Comment: This answer does not talk about the reliability of Interpol as a source of information. It doesn't look at what type of source it is or whether it is expert or informed. This answer hints at the idea of

reputation, but the reputation of a national police force doesn't necessarily apply to Interpol. It also hints at a reason to lie – but there is no good reason for this. Can you improve this answer?

Answer 3: Big international organizations usually have teams of researchers and lawyers who ensure that they get important facts right. Interpol will use correct legal definitions, and they will be well informed about international policing issues including human trafficking. Also, the source gives definitions mostly – why would Interpol lie about definitions of human trafficking? So I think it is quite a reliable source of definitions and information.

Comment: This is a thorough and thoughtful answer. It uses knowledge of big international organizations generally and applies them to Interpol, which is a good exam strategy (even though, in normal life, you would look up Interpol). It is also reasonable to ask why anyone would lie about the kind of information in this document.

The next activity gives more examples of sources of information that you may come across when researching.

> **Remember**
>
> Always question the opinions, predictions, proposals, and value judgments you find in a source. Never accept these just because you think the source is reliable.

Activity 5

(a) In general terms, do you think the following are likely to be reliable sources of facts? Explain your answers.

- **(i)** Supranational organizations like the UN, WHO, and IMF
- **(ii)** Government departments (in various countries)
- **(iii)** Large international charities such as Oxfam, the Red Cross and Red Crescent Societies (IFRC) or Amnesty International.
- **(iv)** The websites of small charities.
- **(v)** Social media pages raising money for good causes.
- **(vi)** The websites of multinational corporations such as Shell, McDonald's, or Siemens
- **(vii)** The websites of small local companies
- **(viii)** Blogs
- **(ix)** Serious newspapers
- **(x)** Sensationalist newspapers

(b) Look at the websites of the organizations and corporations named in part **(a)**.

- **(i)** Find the 'About us' pages. How reliable do they seem? Do they have any particular perspectives or agendas?
- **(ii)** Are there any issues that you think some of these organizations or companies might be less reliable about? Give your reasons.

(c) Look again at the sources used in Activity 3.

- **(i)** Do you think that Press TV from Iran is likely to be a reliable source of information about what Iran's Deputy Ambassador to the UN said? Give your reasons.
- **(ii)** Antislavery.org has a particular agenda on human trafficking. Does this make their story about the girl less reliable? Discuss this.

(d) Go back to your research. Use the questions from Figure 2 to check whether you have chosen reliable sources.

2 Can I trust this information?

So far we have talked about whether we can trust information, ideas, and perspectives in terms of whether the source is reliable. Sometimes you might come across the term "knowledge claims", used instead of information, ideas, and perspectives. This is because these three terms describe things that people *claim* to know. You must check whether you can trust the information in "knowledge claims" by asking these questions:

- Could this be true – is it plausible?

- Can I verify or cross-check this?

- What sort of knowledge claims, information, ideas, or perspectives are there here?

Let's look at some examples of knowledge claims.

In part **(b)** of Activity 4, we looked at an account of a crime at the Treasure jewellery shop, when Darius was accused of the theft. This is the evidence he gave when questioned by the police late on the night of the theft:

> "I left work at about 16.15. It was a really cold evening, so I wrapped up well and put my scarf around my face. Otherwise the cold air gives me a really bad cough. After walking home, I got ready to meet my girlfriend. I took a long time because I was nervous and wanted to look good because I had planned to ask her to marry me. Yes, I bought the ring at Treasure. I went in last week – on Tuesday. No, I didn't go in today; I didn't need to."

How reliable are the claims that Darius makes?
Justify your answer.   [3 marks]

Answer 1: It could easily be true that Darius wrapped up well against the cold, especially if he is not very healthy. This would also explain why he thought he left work at 16.15 but the other report said he left at 16.20 – putting coats and scarves on takes time. It is also plausible that he had already bought the ring, and that he took a long time getting ready because it was an important night. On the other hand, it could also be true that he did in fact spend this time stealing jewellery. Darius's claims are all facts that can be checked. They seem reliable but I would want to check with his parents or flatmates and neighbours whether he was at home – if he was at home, someone probably heard him shutting doors, playing music, or at least taking a shower. I would also want to check whether Darius had a receipt for the ring from last Tuesday.

Comment: This is a long and thoughtful answer, which looks at plausibility, cross-checking and the sorts of information Darius gives. If anything, however, it is too long and too thorough for a three-mark question. Can you improve this answer?

Answer 2: Darius would say that, wouldn't he? If he stole the jewellery, he's going to say that he was somewhere else. But no man is going to take two hours to get ready to go out. He probably stole the ring and pretended to be at home. If the police think he did it, he probably did. But he wouldn't rob a jewellery store. He works in a bank, which would be a much better place to rob.

Comment: This answer is not really dealing with how reliable Darius's claims are. It touches on the idea that Darius would have a reason to lie if he had stolen the jewellery. But otherwise it is more concerned with whether Darius did steal the jewellery. The last sentence seems to contradict the rest of the answer. Can you improve this answer?

In Activity 3 (on page 136), Document 3 gives a migrant domestic worker's account of her friend's bad experiences. How reliable are her knowledge claims? [3 marks]

Answer 1: This girl cannot know for certain what happened to her friend. Her friend might have lied to her, or the girls might have struggled with the language and misunderstood. But I think her story is reliable. Running away from her employer only makes sense if they treat her badly. If someone else gave her the bruises, why run away? And it is possible. In our private homes, people can be very cruel to each other.

Comment: This is a thoughtful answer. It is a good point to say that the girl cannot know what happened to her friend. It is also a good point to consider what makes sense, and what people can be like. This is a kind of cross-checking of facts, using our understanding of people.

Answer 2: It is plausible. We don't like to think of this kind of abuse happening in our country, so we want to say that the girl's story is wrong, but it can happen. We can cross-check with document 1, which says, "They are stripped of their autonomy, freedom of movement and choice, and face various forms of physical and mental abuse."

Comment: This is also a thoughtful answer. cross-checking with Document 1 is a good exam strategy.

Activity 6

(a) How reliable are the knowledge claims in the following documents?

Document 1

> Research indicates that the more foreign aid spent on health, the less the recipient spends – while nearly two-thirds of health spending in Africa was found to be diverted for other uses. One new study just found the biggest improvements in infant survival in Malawi in areas that received less or no aid; meanwhile, Sierra Leone has just indicted its 29 top health officials after funds went astray, despite this being the world's third most dangerous place to give birth.
>
> **Source:** http://www.independent.co.uk/voices/comment/corrupt-ineffective-and-hypocritical-britain-should-give-less-aid-not-more-8599403.html

Document 2

Too often, governments and international agencies have sought to fight the diseases of poverty with aspirational but impractical policies. Millions of dollars and countless working hours have been wasted on ill-conceived and poorly run initiatives, needlessly costing lives.

Source: http://www.policynetwork.net/programs-policy-projects

Document 3

Myth 4. "Aid is useless, due to corruption in the governments who receive it."

The grain of truth:

"Corruption is a big problem in many developing countries and it can sometimes lead to aid money being diverted from its intended purpose."

The full picture:

"While corruption can lessen the impact of aid, it is important to understand that most aid money gets to its proper destination. This is especially true for money that is not given to a foreign government, but is instead directly spent on an aid project. Even taking corruption into account, you can realistically hope to greatly improve the lives of thousands of people through your donations, especially if you donate to programs that don't involve any valuable goods for corrupt officials to divert. Moreover, if you are particularly concerned about the effects of corruption, then you can donate to programs that fight corruption in developing countries."

Source: http://www.givingwhatwecan.org/why-give/myths-about-aid

(b) Go back to your research. Use the questions from Figure 2 to check how reliable the knowledge claims in the documents you have selected are.

3 What about the causes and consequences?

Considering causes and consequences in exam conditions is very much like considering them when you are engaging in research. You ask the same questions:

- Are there alternative possible causes or consequences?
- How likely the predicted consequences?
- Is there any exaggeration, oversimplification or ignoring of other possibilities?

Let's look at an example.

> "A judge has said that we should take babies away from criminal families and get them adopted into law-abiding families. This will prevent future crime and save the nation money."
>
> How reasonable are the causes and consequences suggested?

Answer 1: If crime is caused by being with a criminal family, then taking babies away from criminal families might have the consequence of preventing future crime. But this is oversimplifying the causes of crime. Genetics, poverty, education and politics are all other things that contribute to people becoming criminals. Also, being loved by your real family is important to growing up properly, so taking babies from their real families might not have the positive consequences the judge suggests.

Comment: This is a thoughtful answer. It considers oversimplification and alternative possibilities.

Answer 2: This ignores the possibility that there aren't enough families who would be willing to adopt criminals' children. So the actual consequence might be that these children end up in a care system. As a result they might cost the nation a lot of money, and they might be unloved and unsupported and turn to crime anyway. The judge also ignores other possibilities for helping the children of criminals to live a good life.

Comment: This is also a thoughtful answer. The first part makes a valid practical point, which would mean that the judge's predicted consequence is unlikely. The second part about other possibilities for helping children of criminals is undeveloped – what might these possibilities be?

Answer 3: Sterilization should be mandatory for hardcore thugs. They just shouldn't be allowed to have children. Who wants to grow up knowing their dad's a murderer, anyway? It doesn't matter whether you grow up with your family or not. Just knowing that is going to be enough.

Comment: This answer is giving opinions about how we should deal with criminals' children. It is not considering the reasonableness of the causes and consequences that the judge suggested.

What do you think about the value judgments that underlie this discussion? We will consider value judgments later.

Activity 7

How reasonable are the causes and consequences suggested in the passages below?

(a) "If we can get broadband Internet access to everyone, the economy will improve significantly."

(b) "Aid leads to dependency, corruption, and waste. People who are given free things do not value them as much as people who work for what they have. Furthermore, giving people free things results in them believing they cannot achieve for themselves or that they have no reason to strive for success. Trade can lead to booming economies, higher employment and benefits for both developed and developing countries. So we should clearly promote trade, not aid."

(c) "Aid can be overused, with the consequences of dependency, corruption, and waste. This is true. However, this does not mean that we should abandon aid and rely on trade to improve people's lives. Trade can also lead to negative consequences. Trade is about money, not about improving lives. It can lead to a small number of people becoming very rich, while the majority remain poor. Trade often involves exploitation of the poor. So we need a third option – a humane option that helps people improve their lives without becoming dependent on aid. If we use aid to provide small loans to businesses and to help people use and develop technology such as solar-powered computers, we will combine the advantages of aid and trade, without any of the disadvantages."

(d) Go back to your research. Use the questions from Figure 2 to consider how reasonable the suggested causes and consequences are.

What do you think about the values that underlie these views?

4 How good is the reasoning?

You have already practised evaluating the quality of reasoning during your individual research, by asking the following questions:

- Are reasons given to support an opinion, a conclusion, or a proposal?
- How logical is the reasoning?
- Does it use emotion to persuade me instead of reason?
- Are there gaps in the reasoning?
- Are the facts and evidence used well?

We are going to practise these more now, in the context of the written exam. We are also going to add questions about the values shown. We can ask:

- Do I agree with these values? If so, how far? Completely? Only partly? Only in some circumstances?
- Are they reasonable values?
- Do these values apply in all circumstances?

Activity 8

Working in groups, consider the following values. How far do you agree with them? Think about why. Are some of them reasonable even if you disagree with them? Can you think of circumstances in which they should or should not apply?

(a) An eye for an eye, a tooth for a tooth.

(b) Killing is wrong.

(c) People should work for what they have.

(d) There is nothing wrong with some people being richer than others.

(e) Some people don't deserve to be helped.

(f) People are equal.

(g) The punishment for murder should always be death.

(h) Employers should treat their staff well.

(i) The law should protect all workers from bad employers.

(j) We have a duty to help those less fortunate than ourselves.

Now we will add thinking about values to the other ways of thinking about the quality of reasoning. Let's look at some examples that we have already seen:

> "Sterilization should be mandatory for hardcore thugs. They just shouldn't be allowed to have children. Who wants to grow up knowing their dad's a murderer, anyway? It doesn't matter whether you grow up with your family or not. Just knowing that is going to be enough."

> How good-quality is this reasoning?

Answer: This is not good-quality reasoning. It does not give reasons to support an opinion, a conclusion, or a proposal. It just gives opinions and uses emotion instead of reason to persuade people. It is illogical and unconnected. I think it assumes that the children of criminals will become criminals, even if they are loved and well brought up. There are lots of circumstances in which children of criminals lead ordinary, law-abiding lives. Also, I wonder whether it is reasonable to take away people's human right to have children if they commit crimes. We take away people's liberty, and sometimes their lives. But somehow it seems worse to take away their right to have children. This is a value that needs more thought.

Comment: This is a thoughtful answer, which considers reasons, emotion, gaps in the reasoning, and the values shown.

> "Aid leads to dependency, corruption, and waste. People who are given free things do not value them as much as people who work for what they have. Furthermore, giving people free things results in them believing they cannot achieve for themselves or that they have no reason to strive for success. Trade can lead to booming economies, higher unemployment and benefits for both developed and developing countries. So we should clearly promote trade, not aid."

> How good-quality is this reasoning?

Answer: This passage overstates the positive consequences of trade and exaggerates the negative consequences of aid. It ignores the good consequences of aid and the bad consequences of trade. So it isn't logical to conclude that we should promote trade, not aid. Also, it assumes that the bad consequences happen all the time. But sometimes helping people, giving them things, can be the right thing to do. It can give them the confidence to help themselves.

Comment: This answer is thoughtful but only partly successful. It makes good use of thinking about consequences to show that the reasoning isn't logical. Towards the end it starts to argue against the reasoning, expressing its own opinion rather than evaluating the reasoning. Can you improve the last part?

Activity 9

How good-quality is the reasoning in the following passages? Explain your answers.

(a) "According to the OECD [Organisation for Economic Co-operation and Development], development aid fell by 4 per cent in 2012, following a fall of 2 per cent in 2011. This shows that countries have recognized that aid isn't needed any more."

(b) "We can't go on pouring billions of dollars into the pockets of foreign dictators who don't respect human rights. We are slashing the budgets for the armed forces, health, and education in our own country. Projects to get our young people into work or training are being cut. So let's welcome the proposal to use aid money to get our national companies investing in infrastructure in developing countries, instead of just giving it to corrupt governments."

(c) "New technology is supposed to create employment. But I don't believe it. They brought new machines and robots into our factory, and now most of us are unemployed. We want to work, but they don't need us. What are ordinary people supposed to do? We're trapped between employers who'd rather use robots, and a government that tells us to find work but doesn't help us, and people who believe we're lazy because we haven't got jobs."

Reflect and plan

The next stage is to reflect on the issues, ideas, and perspectives that you have considered so far. You will also start to reflect on the learning process you use in Global Perspectives.

Activity 10

Here are some questions to think about. Let them float around in your mind over the next few days. Keep coming back to them.

(a) What are the values that matter to you? Why?

(b) What sort of world do you want to live in? Why?

Activity 11

(a) Use a diagram or mind map to help you reflect on the links between the four topics in this section:

- Employment
- Technology and the economic divide
- Law and criminality
- Trade and aid

(b) How does your personal perspective on these issues link to different national and global perspectives?

(c) What is the most important issue that you have considered so far in this section?

(d) Can you think of any links between these topics and the other topics you have considered so far during this course? Think back to the topics you looked at in Sections 1, 2 and 3.

Activity 12

As a result of humankind's poor choices, the earth is dying. Scientists have found an earth-like planet and developed the technology to transport 1,000 people there. There are just two problems. About 25 per cent of the people will catch a local disease. With proper health care, 90 per cent of these will recover but, without healthcare, 60 per cent will be left with active minds but serious physical disabilities. The second problem is that the settlers might have to deal with intelligent beings that already live on the planet – scientists are not sure.

(a) You need to decide how you are going to select 1,000 volunteers. What characteristics do you want your settlers to have?

(b) You need to decide what kind of society to have in the new world. Think about which values are important and write three or four basic laws for each of the areas shown in this table.

Area	Questions to ask
Government	• What balance do you want between individual freedom and community strength? • Will decisions be made democratically, autocratically, communally, or by some other form of government? • Is equality important in your society? Think about equality in terms of rights, wealth, and the opportunity to do well, for example.
Resources, energy	• Will resources be jointly owned by all 1,000 settlers, or divided in some other way? • What precautions will you take to avoid the overuse of resources?
Employment and the economy	• Will everyone work for themselves or will some of the settlers employ others? How will this be decided? • Will you have a system of money or not? If so, why, and if not, what sort of economy will you have?
Healthcare and aid	• What sort of healthcare provision will you have? Will people pay each time they need healthcare or will the community group together to ensure that everyone gets healthcare when they need it? Remember the local illness that will strike 25 per cent of the people, and the likelihood of accidents. • How will the community help those who have bad luck or who do badly? Will there be "aid" for those who struggle?
Crime	• What basic laws will you have to prevent crime? • How will you deal with criminals?

Reflecting on how you learn

So far you have mostly reflected on the range of topic-based issues covered in Global Perspectives. In order to take your skills to the next stage, you need to reflect on the new ways of learning you have developed on the course.

Activity 13

(a) Make a list of all the differences between Global Perspectives learning and other learning you do.

(b) What do you like about the Global Perspectives way of learning? Why?

(c) What do you find difficult? Why? How can you improve in this area?

(d) How independent are you when you are learning?

(e) What skills do you use when you plan a line of inquiry?

(f) Do you remember to use your information to answer a question or support a proposal or decision?

(g) Do you select only relevant information?

(h) What do you need the teacher to help you with?

Planning and evaluating project work

When you do your assessed project work, you will need to submit:

- your plan
- a group report, including evidence of the process and outcome
- an individual evaluation.

You need to take this into consideration when you are planning and managing your project. This will help you produce what you need as you go along. For example, you could:

- take photographs of meetings and activities
- record conversations
- print a copy of relevant emails, receipts, and other documents
- reflect on your own performance – for example, if you argue with a team-mate, ask, "How could I have dealt with that better? What strategies will I use if we have a similar situation again?" You could write down your thoughts, so that you have things to say when you have to write your individual evaluation.

Activity 14

(a) What does SMART mean?

(b) What are the different stages of the project planning and evaluation process? (Refer back to Section 3 if you can't remember.)

(c) You are producing a short play for your local community, to raise money to support a centre that counsels victims of human trafficking. What do you think would be useful evidence of

  (i) the planning and management process?

  (ii) the outcome (the play or the raised money)?

(d) You are collaborating with a group of students from a school on a different continent, working on issues to do with technology and the economic divide.

  (i) What would be a SMART outcome that would be suitable for this international group?

  (ii) How would you show evidence of your cross-cultural collaboration?

  (iii) What sort of evidence would show the project planning and management process?

  (iv) What sort of evidence would demonstrate the outcome you have decided on?

Individual evaluation

When you do your individual evaluation of a project, use the questions in the table below to help you.

Individual evaluation	
My role	What was my role?
	What was my individual contribution?
	What have I learned about working with others (overseas)?
	What were my strong points?
The outcome	Was the outcome successful? For example, did the event raise awareness and money?
	Were there enough links to the issue – did we succeed in our primary aim – or was it just a good experience that failed to achieve the primary aim?
The team	What were the team's strong points?
	How was my teamwork?
	How was our organization?
	How was our time management?
	How was the leadership?
Problems and solutions	What were our difficulties?
	How did we overcome the difficulties?
	How did I contribute to solving difficulties?
	What could we have done to prevent the difficulties?
	How could we better have solved the difficulties?
Personal reflection	What have I learned from the process?
	How will I improve next time?

In Sections 1, 2 and 3 you did a project or a mini project.

(a) How successful were these projects? Use the questions in the table above to help you with your evaluation.

(b) How would you improve the projects you have done if you could do them again?

(c) What do you personally need to improve in your planning, your teamwork, your management, and getting things done?

(d) How will you go about making these improvements in the next project you do?

Present and take action

So far you have worked on presenting your own logical argument, and now you are going to consider how to include different perspectives or viewpoints, and how to present your project.

Including other perspectives

When you present an argument, you give reasons and evidence to support your view. It is also often useful to show why you disagree with other views or perspectives. When you do this, you need to:

- take the other view seriously and respect the people who hold it

- look at the reasons or evidence for the other view

- say why you disagree, show why the other view is wrong, or find a compromise.

You already know how to use words like *because, also, so, therefore,* to link your ideas. When you are showing why you disagree with another view, you can use phrases like:

- Some people believe that…

- It is sometimes argued that…

- An alternative perspective on this issue is…

- However…

- On the other hand…

- This is true but…

- There is another way of seeing this…

Let's look at some examples.

Is it ever right for workers to strike?

In your answer you should:

- give reasons for your opinion;
- use relevant examples to support your opinion (you may use your own experience);
- show that you have considered different points of view;
- explain why you disagreed with some of these points of view.

(Cambridge IGCSE Global Perspectives, 0457, May/June 2011, Paper 3, Q8)

Answer 1: Striking is always wrong because it causes chaos and havoc. When bus drivers are striking, people can't get to work, so they don't earn any money. It is also selfish of the bus drivers, because they are lucky to have a job and shouldn't be demanding more money. Teachers at our school went on strike last year just before the exams. Students who had exams were worried, and felt that they should be getting more support from the teachers. My mother was angry, because she had to stay at home with my little brother, who was too young to be alone. This meant she didn't get paid, and her boss was unhappy with her. If you have a job you should do your job.

Comment: This response does answer the question, and does give reasons and examples to support the conclusion. But the conclusion – that striking is "always wrong" – is too extreme, so the argument isn't completely logical. The answer looks at the views of students and a parent, but not at the views or perspectives of the striking bus drivers or teachers.

Answer 2: Some people think that striking is wrong. They think it is selfish. Other people think that striking is right if your boss doesn't treat you properly. I think that striking is sometimes selfish and sometimes right.

Comment: This response attempts to include different perspectives, but just states different views. It is not really thinking about them, or trying to understand why people think what they think. It gives no reasons. This is a very simple attempt.

Answer 3: Some people think that striking is selfish because, when people don't do their jobs, it can have a bad effect on other people. It is true that striking can affect other people, such as when bus drivers go on strike and people can't get to work, or when air stewards go on strike and people can't travel.

But you could also argue that it is selfish of the public to put our own concerns ahead of the needs of the bus drivers and the air stewards. We could perhaps ask whether our holiday or business trip is so important. Furthermore, striking can be the most effective way to stop a company exploiting workers. If people band together they can achieve great improvements in working conditions. For example, if people are working 18-hour days in bad light and don't get toilet breaks, it is reasonable to strike to improve conditions.

On the other hand, there are circumstances when striking is wrong. If you earn a reasonable wage, like doctors, and if people would die because you are striking for more money, then the strike is wrong. But last year in my country, doctors went on strike because the government was making bad decisions about health care. The doctors made sure that all emergencies would be treated, but only emergencies. So no one died, but some people were inconvenienced. This made the whole country realize that the government was making bad decisions, and this was not a selfish strike. So overall, I think that it is sometimes right to strike, but not always, and it is important to think about the circumstances carefully.

Comment: This is a very thoughtful response. It is mostly well structured, mostly logical, and takes different views seriously. It gives reasons and examples, and the conclusion follows logically from the argument.

Activity 16

(a) Do you think Western governments should continue to give aid to developing countries? Give reasons for your answer and consider at least one different view.

(b) Do you think that Darius was the Treasure robber? Consider the evidence on pages 140 and 144 and write an argument to support your view. Consider at least one different view.

(c) Propose one national and one international action that can be taken against human traffickers. Explain how they would work and write an argument to persuade your government to agree to them. Consider at least one different view.

(d) You are the leader of a remote village in an underdeveloped area. You are discussing with a charity how to invest in your community. The options under discussion are:

- providing small loans to women to operate small businesses
- educating one child from each family in solar-powered communications technology
- co-operating with a multinational corporation in a large infrastructure project.

Write an argument to persuade the villages to accept one of these options or another option of your choice. Explain why you do not support the other options.

Presenting your group project

Presenting your project documents is different from presenting arguments and explanations in a research report or exam answer. You will be providing evidence of a planning, management and evaluation process. More information on presenting your group project is available on www.oxfordsecondary.co.uk/gp.

> ### Remember
>
> In your documents, use:
>
> ▶ headings
>
> ▶ bullets
>
> ▶ lists, tables and diagrams
>
> ▶ posters, photographs and other images.
>
> Always include records of your conversations, telephone calls, and emails.

Section 4
13 Employment

In this section you will complete a research report and a group project, and do a practice written paper. You should now be working fairly independently and meeting most of the assessment criteria in your work. Remember that you can still ask your teacher for guidance, and discuss important issues with him or her. You can also refer to any of the skills development activities in this book as you work.

Individual research

> If you do decide to submit work from this section for assessment, come back and check it again after you have worked through Section 5.

Activity 13.1

(a) Remind yourself of the key stages of planning an inquiry.

(b) Choose an issue relating to employment that interests you.

(c) Set a question.

(d) Research, question, and reflect.

(e) Remind yourself of the precise assessment requirements for a research report.

    (i) Remember to consider a problem, its causes and consequences, different perspectives, possible solutions, and the consequences of these possible solutions.

    (ii) Remember that you need to develop a line of reasoning – using your research to help you support a conclusion, decision, or proposal for action.

(f) Write your research report.

> You can choose your own question, but here are some ideas:
>
> - What is the best way to deal with the problems of youth unemployment?
>
> - Should governments prioritise local job creation or encourage trade with multinational corporations?

> **Remember**
>
> A good question will:
>
> ▶ give you focus
>
> ▶ require you to develop a line of reasoning (this means justifying opinions and values, not just describing)
>
> ▶ help you meet the assessment requirements, including looking at problems, their causes and consequences, possible solutions, and different perspectives.

> Look back at the feedback you received on previous research reports. What do you need to improve on? How will you improve it this time?

Group project

Activity 13.2

(a) Form a group and remind yourselves of the key stages in planning, managing and carrying out a project.

(b) Discuss with your teacher how you can collaborate with people from another country or culture.

(c) Set an outcome.

(d) Remind yourselves of the precise assessment requirements.

(e) Plan, manage and carry out your project.

(f) Evaluate your project, and produce relevant documentation.

You can choose your own project outcome, but here are some ideas:

- Set up a working group with unemployed people in your local area. Use surveys, interviews and conversations to find out what their needs are. Either

    (a) produce a report for your local leaders

    (b) work with people to help them improve their IT (or other) skills and report back to your school or

    (c) write an article for your local newspaper (and get it published).

- Interview and survey local employers to find out what skills and activities they are looking for in young employees. Compare your results with those of students from a partner school in a different country (or a classmate with a different cultural background from yours). Produce a report (with graphs, diagrams etc.) for students in your school.

> Is your outcome SMART?

> Look back at previous self-evaluations. What do you need to improve on? How can you improve this time?

> **Remember**
>
> Always respect other people's traditions and cultures.

Written exam practice

Document 1

"I JUST DON'T GET IT. I'VE APPLIED FOR OVER 200 JOBS, BUT I'VE NEVER EVEN GOT A CALL BACK."

Document 2

Thread: rude colleague

@sadandunhappy: "I'm having problems with a colleague at work and I want some advice on how to deal with him. John is rude and unpleasant most of the time – a lot of it is just little things, like he'll stand in the doorway and not let me through, or make comments about my personal hygiene. The thing is, I do quite a lot of his job as well as my own, but our boss doesn't realize this. She believes John when he says that I am lazy. For example, I came in at 10 a.m. after seeing a client, and John said, 'What time do you call this? Can't you get to work on time and help those of us doing the real work?' I'm getting more and more stressed and I don't even want to go to work any more."

@juniperberry: "Well, you could try having a wash, turning up on time and doing your fair share of the work. If you were actually doing your share of work your boss would notice. This country is suffering a real decline in productivity because of layabouts like you, who don't pull their weight. This is going to lead to economic recession and unemployment, and that will cause a huge rise in the crime rate. So do some work and stop being so sad and unhappy."

@teeniusgenius: "I think you're being unfair, **@juniperberry**. Teachers don't always notice who is working hard and who is messing around – they have their favourites and some of them make judgments based on what they already think about people, not on what people are actually doing. So why not bosses? **@sadandunhappy**, I had a similar situation in my part-time job this summer. I think you should try having a calm chat with your boss and explaining the situation. Ask for advice about how to deal with the situation rather than being personal and complaining, because this is more likely to get results."

@hairyjumper: "I think you should treat your colleague just exactly the way he treats you, **@sadandunhappy**. Be rude, be strong, and make sure you keep telling the boss just what a loser this John is. And stop doing his work. This will make both him and your boss realize how much you are actually doing."

@diamondlight: "**@sadandunhappy**, talk to your boss in a calm way. I work in human resources, and I see this all the time, the way people's perspectives are skewed by fear and uncertainty and partial information. If you explain your perspective to your boss, she will make a better decision because she will have more evidence."

Question 1

Consider Document 1.

(a) What employment issues does the cartoon raise? [3 marks]

(b) Explain how and why the perspectives of the teenager and the employment adviser might be different. [3 marks]

Consider Document 2.

(c) Identify three possible solutions to **@sadandunhappy's** problem. [3 marks]

(d) To what extent do you think this problem can be explained by different perspectives? Justify your answer. [3 marks]

Question 2

(a) **@sadandunhappy** says his boss "believes John when he says that I am lazy". What evidence would you need to decide whether this is true? [4 marks]

(b) How would you research this evidence? [2 marks]

(c) **@juniperberry** believes that **@sadandunhappy** "could try having a wash, turning up on time and doing your fair share of the work". What evidence would you need to decide whether **@sadandunhappy** does need to do these things or whether John is being rude and unfair? [4 marks]

(d) How would this evidence help you make the decision? [2 marks]

Question 3

(a) How reliable is **@teeniusgenius** as a source of advice for **@sadandunhappy**? Explain your answer. [3 marks]

(b) How good is **@juniperberry's** reasoning? [6 marks]

In your answers, consider some of the following:

● Are reasons given to support an opinion/conclusion/proposal?

● How logical is the reasoning?

● Does the speaker use emotion to persuade me instead of reason?

● Are there gaps in the reasoning?

● Are the facts and evidence used well?

(c) How likely are the consequences suggested by **@juniperberry**, **@teeniusgenius** and **@hairyjumper**? [9 marks]

Question 4

How well does modern education prepare young people for work in today's global economy? [18 marks]

In your answer, you should:

● state your conclusion

● give reasons

● give examples where relevant

● show that you have considered at least one other viewpoint.

Section 4

14 Technology and the economic divide

In this section you will complete a research report and a group project, and do a practice written paper. You should now be working fairly independently and meeting most of the assessment criteria in your work. Remember that you can still ask your teacher for guidance, and discuss important issues with him or her. You can also refer to any of the skills development activities in this book as you work.

Individual research

> If you do decide to submit work from this section for assessment, come back and check it again after you have worked through Section 5.

Activity 14.1

(a) Remind yourself of the key stages of planning an inquiry.

(b) Choose an issue relating to technology and the economic divide that interests you.

(c) Set a question.

(d) Research, question, and reflect.

(e) Remind yourself of the precise assessment requirements for a research report.

  (i) Remember to consider a problem, its causes and consequences, different perspectives, possible solutions, and the consequences of these possible solutions.

  (ii) Remember that you need to develop a line of reasoning – using your research to help you support a conclusion, decision, or proposal for action.

(f) Write your research report.

You can choose your own question, but here are some ideas:
- How can we provide high-quality Internet access to the majority?
- How important is technology to economic and social progress?

Remember

A good question will:
- give you focus
- require you to develop a line of reasoning (this means justifying opinions and values, not just describing)
- help you meet the assessment requirements, including looking at problems, their causes and consequences, possible solutions, and different perspectives.

Look back at the feedback you received on previous research reports. What do you need to improve on? How will you improve it this time?

Group project

Activity 14.2

(a) Form a group and remind yourselves of the key stages in planning, managing, and carrying out a project.

(b) Discuss with your teacher how you can collaborate with people from another country or culture.

(c) Set an outcome.

(d) Remind yourselves of the precise assessment criteria for a group project.

(e) Plan, manage, and carry out your project.

(f) Evaluate your project.

> You can choose your own project outcome, but here are some ideas:
>
> - Working with a partner school from another country (or with classmates who have lived in another country), compare the technologies used by different social groups in your two countries. Produce a documentary on how much these differences affect the countries.
>
> - Set up a working group to teach older people how to use computers/mobile phones/the Internet.

Is your outcome SMART?

Look back at previous self-evaluations. What do you need to improve on? How can you improve this time?

Remember

Always respect other people's traditions and cultures.

Written exam practice

Document 1

Should we use technology to enhance performance?

@healthyathlete: "No, as Francis Fukuyama said: 'The original purpose of medicine is to heal the sick, not turn healthy people into gods.'"

@honestjack: "No, using technology is cheating. In sport we want to watch natural athletes who have worked hard and made sacrifices to be the best. Popping pills or using technology just isn't fair play, and it will lead to a competition between engineers and surgeons instead of sportspeople. We could end up with them building weapons into people's arms and legs."

@technokid: "This is ridiculous. Training regimes use technology; sports shoes use technology. Where would we be in motor racing without technology? Still racing chariots behind horses? For most international competitions you couldn't even get to the playing field without the technology used in aeroplanes. If we accept medical technology, we will extend the limits of what it is to be human. This could be very exciting."

@tiredandoverworked: "Would I use brain stimulation to keep me awake to finish the assignment I'm working on? Oh, yes. Brain stimulation will give us all the benefits of medical stimulation without the side effects. It will transform the way we work."

@silverbirch: "This is oversimplifying the issue. Brain stimulation has disadvantages as well as advantages. For example, a study done at Oxford University found that if you stimulate one area of the brain, you can learn mathematical concepts more quickly – but the disadvantage is that you become less good at applying the new concepts. If you stimulate a different area of the brain, you learn the new concepts more slowly, but then you are much better at applying the new concepts. And, as yet, we know nothing about the long-term consequences. So we should be cautious.

@jasminetea: "Another thing to consider is that we all know that a stimulating environment can help young people learn. But experiments on rats have shown that this stimulating environment can change the structure of the brain. So is this enhancement?

Document 2

US military researchers have had great success using "transcranial direct current stimulation" (tDCS) – in which they let electrical current flow through your brain. tDCS can more than double the rate at which people learn a wide range of tasks, such as object recognition, math skills, and marksmanship.

Is brain boosting fair? Will it create a social divide, where the rich can afford to be smarter and everyone else will be left behind? Will Tiger Moms force their lazy kids to strap on a zappity helmet during piano practice?

After trying it myself, I have different questions. To make you understand, I am going to tell you how it felt. To start with, I found the marksmanship task difficult, and I became obsessed with my failure. But with the electrodes on, my constant self-criticism virtually disappeared and I was able to complete the marksmanship task.

If you told me tDCS would allow someone to study twice as fast for the bar exam, I might be worried because I have visions of rich daddies paying for Junior's thinking cap. But now think of a different application — could school-age girls use the zappy cap while studying math to drown out the voices that tell them they can't do math because they're girls?

And then, finally, the main question: What role do doubt and fear play in our lives if their eradication actually causes so many improvements? Do we make more ethical decisions when we listen to our inner voices of self-doubt or when we're freed from them? If we all wore these caps, would the world be a better place?

©2012 by Sally Adee, reprinted by permission of New Scientist. The full article can be found at NewScientist.com.

Source: http://theweek.com/article/index/226196/how-electrical-brain-stimulation-can-change-the-way-we-think

Question 1

(a) Give three reasons for using technological enhancements   [3 marks]

(b) Give three reasons against using technological enhancements   [3 marks]

(c) Is technological enhancement mostly a personal, national or global issue?   [6 marks]

Question 2

(a) **@silverbirch** talks about an experiment in which areas of the brain are stimulated one at a time.

How would you find out what would happen if two or more areas were stimulated at the same time? What problems would you encounter if you tried?   [6 marks]

(b) Sally Adee, the author of Document 2, asks, "Do we make more ethical decisions when we listen to our inner voices of self-doubt or when we're freed from them?"

Suggest an experiment that would help you to find the answer to this question. What problems would you expect to encounter?   [6 marks]

Question 3

(a) "The original purpose of medicine is to heal the sick, not turn healthy people into gods." Is this a fact, an opinion, a prediction or a value judgment? Explain your answer.   [3 marks]

(b) **@silverbirch** mentions a study done at Oxford University. Is this a reliable source of information? Explain your answer.   [3 marks]

(c) Does **@honestjack** predict likely consequences? Justify your answer.   [3 marks]

(d) **@honestjack** expresses the value that, "Popping pills or using technology just isn't fair play."

Do you accept this value? Justify your answer.   [3 marks]

(e) How good is **@technokid**'s reasoning? Justify your answer.   [3 marks]

(f) How good is **@silverbirch**'s reasoning? Justify your answer.   [3 marks]

Question 4

Are there some areas of life in which we should reject technological enhancement in order to increase fairness?   [18 marks]

In your answer, you should:

- state your conclusion
- give reasons
- give examples, where relevant
- show that you have considered at least one other viewpoint.

Section 4
15 Law and criminality

In this section you will complete a research report and a group project, and do a practice written paper. You should now be working fairly independently and meeting most of the assessment criteria in your work. Remember that you can still ask your teacher for guidance, and discuss important issues with him or her. You can also refer to any of the skills development activities in this book as you work.

> If you do decide to submit work from this section for assessment, come back and check it again after you have worked through Section 5.

Individual research

Activity 15.1

(a) Remind yourself of the key stages of planning an inquiry.

(b) Choose an issue relating to law and criminality that interests you.

(c) Set a question.

(d) Research, question and reflect.

(e) Remind yourself of the precise assessment requirements for a research report.

    (i) Remember to consider a problem, its causes and consequences, different perspectives, possible solutions, and the consequences of these possible solutions.

    (ii) Remember that you need to develop a line of reasoning – using your research to help you support a conclusion, decision, or proposal for action.

(f) Write your research report.

> You can choose your own question, but here are some ideas:
>
> • What are the best ways to deal with international/cross border crime?
>
> • Should all countries have the same laws?

Remember

A good question will:

▶ give you focus

▶ require you to develop a line of reasoning (this means justifying opinions and values, not just describing)

▶ help you meet the assessment requirements, including looking at problems, their causes and consequences, possible solutions, and different perspectives.

> Look back at the feedback you received on previous research reports. What do you need to improve on? How will you improve it this time?

Group project

Activity 15.2

(a) Form a group and remind yourselves of the key stages in planning, managing, and carrying out a project.

(b) Discuss with your teacher how you can collaborate with people from another country or culture.

(c) Set an outcome.

> Is your outcome SMART?

(d) Remind yourselves of the precise assessment requirements.

(e) Plan, manage, and carry out your project.

(f) Evaluate your project.

> Look back at previous self-evaluations. What do you need to improve on? How can you improve this time?

You can choose your own project outcome, but here are some ideas:

- Research the law (and punishments for breaking it) in your country in one particular area – e.g. age limits, property and theft, immigration or murder/manslaughter. Work with students from a partner school who have researched the law in their country in the same area. Alternatively, you could work with classmates who have lived in another country. Compare the differences and the different consequences. Produce a report (with graphs, diagrams etc.) or an article for local newspapers.

- "It is illegal to die in the Houses of Parliament in London." "In Florida it is illegal for unmarried women to parachute on Sundays." Work with students from a partner school in a different country to research bizarre laws. What were the causes and consequences of these laws? What were the different perspectives that led to them being made? Produce a video explaining and analysing these causes, consequences and perspectives.

> **Remember**
>
> Always respect other people's traditions and cultures.

Written exam practice

Document 1

Gun murder compared by country

Top 10 countries

By rate per 100,000 people

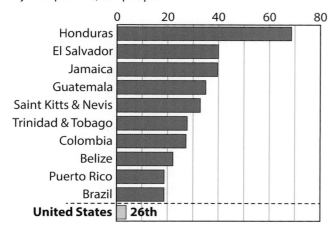

Source: UNODC, Latest data for each country (2004–2010)

Developed countries*

Rate per 100,000 people

*Listed in Human Development index order

Document 2

DAILY OUTRAGE

Public outrage as judges pass unfair sentences

Our criminal justice system has been called into question today by the punishments handed down by judges in three different cases.

Case 1
Person: Banker
Offence: Fraud. He was convicted of using $10 million of clients' money to fund his own extravagant lifestyle.
Plea: Guilty
Sentence: 15 months in prison

Case 2
Person: Migrant agricultural worker
Offence: Armed burglary. He was convicted of breaking into and entering the home of a millionaire with a gun and stealing $50 000 worth of valuables.
Plea: Not guilty
Sentence: 10 years in prison

Case 3
Person: Farmer
Offence: Shooting and killing a burglar
Plea: Not guilty
Sentence: 15 years in prison

What do you think? Are these sentences fair?

@amazinggrace: "This just shows what this country is coming to when you can't even defend your home any more. It's the burglar who should be sent to prison, not the person he burgled. There's no hope for us in this day and age. It's like that case where the teenager sued a business because he fell through their roof, and the judge said the business should have kept the roof safe for burglars. It's being so soft on kids that leads to all this crime. What I say is, spare the rod and spoil the child – but these days they'll lock you up for trying to instil proper discipline into your kids."

@be reasonable: "Defending your home is acceptable, but killing the intruder is a bit extreme. Why not just shoot him in the knees so he can't run away and then call the police?"

@hope for the future: "The real outrage is that the rich banker who stole $10 million got 15 months but the poor agricultural worker got 10 years for stealing much less. This is social inequality at its worst. Fraud and burglary are both forms of theft and the punishment should reflect the amount stolen. This would lead to a fairer criminal justice system. We should pay bankers and agricultural workers the same amount of money. This would lead to less greed, a happier society and much less crime."

@cynicalrealist: "You are naive and wrong on two counts, @hope for the future. First, if bankers aren't happy with the millions they already get, how would paying them less reduce their greed? Second, there's an important difference between using a computer to move money that doesn't really exist from one bank account to another, and invading someone's private home with a gun, going through their things and stealing things they really care about."

@innocentbanker: "Not all bankers are greedy and not all of us take criminal actions or make irresponsible decisions. Personally, I think that the criminal, irresponsible few should be punished much more harshly. This is partly because it would make other bankers realize they can't get away with crime, and partly because it gives us all a bad name when criminal bankers seem to get away with it. We should make it quite clear that they are criminals just as much as burglars are. If you break the law you are a criminal. And fraud is breaking the law."

Question 1

Consider Document 1.

(a) Which country has the highest gun crime rate? [1 mark]

(b) Which country has the lowest gun crime rate? [1 mark]

(c) Suggest one reason for the difference in gun crime rate between the countries with the lowest and highest rates. [1 mark]

Consider Document 2.

(d) Explain briefly why the three sentences have caused outrage. Use your own words but refer to the article and online comments. [6 marks]

(e) Identify three possible solutions for the future that are mentioned in the online comments. [3 marks]

Question 2

The migrant agricultural worker claims that he is not guilty of the armed burglary, but he was convicted because one of his hairs was found at the crime scene.

Suggest two pieces of evidence that would help to show that he was in fact not guilty. How would this evidence help? [12 marks]

Question 3

(a) **@be reasonable** says, "Defending your home is acceptable, but killing the intruder is a bit extreme.'"

Do you think this is a fact, an opinion, a prediction or a value judgment? Explain your answer. [3 marks]

(b) How likely are the consequences suggested by **@hope for the future**? Justify your answer. [3 marks]

(c) **@cynicalrealist** says, "there's an important difference between using a computer to move money that doesn't really exist from one bank account to another, and invading someone's private home with a gun, going through their things and stealing things they really care about".

Do you accept this value judgment? Justify your answer. [3 marks]

(d) Whose reasoning is better: **@amazinggrace's** or **@innocentbanker's**? [9 marks]

In your answers, consider some of of the following:

● Are reasons given to support an opinion/conclusion/proposal?

● Is the reasoning logical?

● Does the speaker use emotion to persuade me instead of reason?

● Are there gaps in the reasoning?

● Are the facts and evidence used well?

Question 4

Should anybody be able to legally own a gun? [18 marks]

In your answer, you should:

● state your conclusion

● give reasons

● give examples where relevant

● show that you have considered at least one other viewpoint.

Section 4
16 Trade and aid

In this section you will complete a research report and a group project, and do a practice written paper. You should now be working fairly independently and meeting most of the assessment criteria in your work. Remember that you can still ask your teacher for guidance, and discuss important issues with him or her. You can also refer to any of the skills development activities in this book as you work.

Individual research

If you do decide to submit work from this section for assessment, come back and check it again after you have worked through Section 5.

Activity 16.1

(a) Remind yourself of the key stages of planning an inquiry.

(b) Choose an issue relating to trade and aid that interests you.

(c) Set a question.

(d) Research, question and reflect.

(e) Remind yourself of the precise assessment requirements for a research report.

    (i)   Remember to consider a problem, its causes and consequences, different perspectives, possible solutions, and the consequences of these possible solutions.

    (ii) Remember that you need to develop a line of reasoning – using your research to help you support a conclusion, decision, or proposal for action.

(f) Write your research report.

> You can choose your own question, but here are some ideas:
>
> ● How can we (individuals and states) best help those who are less fortunate than ourselves?
>
> ● "We should concentrate trade and aid on our own country first and work with other countries only if we have resources to spare." How far do you agree with this statement?

Remember

A good question will:

▶ give you focus

▶ require you to develop a line of reasoning (this means justifying opinions and values, not just describing)

▶ help you meet the assessment requirements, including looking at problems, their causes and consequences, possible solutions, and different perspectives.

Look back at the feedback you received on previous research reports. What do you need to improve on? How will you improve it this time?

Group project

(a) Form a group and remind yourselves of the key stages in planning, managing, and carrying out a project.

(b) Discuss with your teacher how you can collaborate with people from another country or culture.

(c) Set an outcome.

(d) Remind yourselves of the precise assessment requirements.

(e) Plan, manage, and carry out your project.

(f) Evaluate your project.

> You can choose your own project outcome, but here are some ideas:
>
> - Set up a small company. Run it for six months and try to make a profit. You will need a business plan and a budget. You could make and sell cakes/craft/jewellery, for example. To include cross-cultural collaboration you could import and sell (typical local) crafts made by students at your partner school, whilst exporting your own crafts to them. Produce a report for your head teacher or an article for your school magazine or local newspaper.
>
> - Work with a deprived community in your own country. Set a project outcome relating to local conditions.

Is your outcome SMART?

Look back at previous self-evaluations. What do you need to improve on? How can you improve this time?

Remember

Always respect other people's traditions and cultures.

Written exam practice

Document 1

Document 2

Kofi Eliasa used to own a tomato farm, but now he breaks stones in a quarry for a living, earning less than a dollar a day to feed his family. He is one of the many farmers in Ghana who have fallen victim to cheap European food imports that have flooded his country ever since the Ghanaian government was forced to open up its markets in return for loans and aid from the IMF and the World Bank.

The problem

It's all part of a wider global picture in which unfair trade rules designed largely by rich countries work against the interests of poor communities in developing countries. While international trade is worth $10 million a minute, poor countries only account for 0.4 per cent of this trade – half the share they had in 1980.

What we do

Here at Christian Aid, we believe that trade must be used to help bring an end to poverty – not deepen and prolong it.

Therefore, we are demanding that:

- the IMF and World Bank remove all economic policy conditions attached to their loans and debt-cancellation agreements.

- World Trade Organization agreements support development rather than promote free trade for the sake of free trade.

Source: http://www.christianaid.org.uk/whatwedo/issues/trade.aspx

Document 3

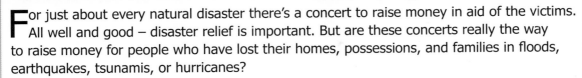

For just about every natural disaster there's a concert to raise money in aid of the victims. All well and good – disaster relief is important. But are these concerts really the way to raise money for people who have lost their homes, possessions, and families in floods, earthquakes, tsunamis, or hurricanes?

@musiclover: "Disaster concerts are a great way to raise money quickly for a good cause. A celebrity could donate $1 million, but by organizing a concert they can raise so much more. And maybe we're selfish, but we get to feel good because we've done some good, as well as hearing some great music."

@cynicalrealist: "Yeah, but how much of that money ends up as aid to the people who need it? And how much in the artist's offshore bank account? Disaster concerts distract from real charity. First of all, it's just wrong to sing and dance and have fun when people are mourning their families, so really, it's all about us and our enjoyment and not about the people we are supposed to be helping. And secondly, celebrities are not the right people to be leading charity campaigns. Non-governmental organizations and registered charities should be doing this."

@cherryblossom: "People like @cynical realist should crawl back to their hole where they came from. Attacking people who come out to support charity is a new low."

@peace not war: "I would rather just give a donation to the Red Cross or Red Crescent. At least with the RC, I am more comfortable that they are not in it for their own glorification."

Question 1

Choose two of the cartoons from Document 1.

(a) Explain the personal, national and global perspectives that arise from one cartoon. You may use diagrams to help you.   [6 marks]

(b) Explain the issues that arise from the other cartoon. You may use diagrams to help you.   [6 marks]

Question 2

There has been a serious earthquake in your country. You have $500 to donate to the relief efforts. You are considering two options, a disaster relief concert and The Red Cross/Red Crescent.

What do you need to know about each of these, and how will this help you decide how to donate your money?

(a) disaster relief concert   [6 marks]

(b) Red Cross/Red Crescent   [6 marks]

Question 3

(a) Document 2 says, "It's all part of a wider global picture in which unfair trade rules designed largely by rich countries work against the interests of poor communities in developing countries."

Is this a fact, an opinion, a prediction or a value judgment?
Explain your answer. [3 marks]

(b) Is **http://www.christianaid.org.uk/whatwedo/issues/trade.aspx** a reliable source regarding trade and aid issues?
Explain your answer. [3 marks]

(c) Whose reasoning is better, **@musiclover**'s or **@cynicalrealist**'s?
Justify your answer. [9 marks]

In your answer, consider some of of the following:

● Are reasons given to support an opinion/conclusion/proposal?

● How logical is the reasoning?

● Does the speaker use emotion to persuade me instead of reason?

● Are there gaps in the reasoning?

● Are the facts and evidence used well?

(d) How effectively does **@cherryblossom** answer **@cynicalrealist**? [3 marks]

Question 4

"Aid is like putting a sticking plaster on a badly broken leg.
We need to treat the causes of poverty, inequality, and injustice rather than the symptoms." Do you agree? [18 marks]

In your answer, you should:

● state your conclusion

● give reasons

● give examples where relevant

● show that you have considered at least one other viewpoint.

Section 5
Skills development activities

You should now be feeling confident about starting to plan a line of inquiry for your research reports. In this section you will be developing your skills and increasing your ability to work independently, using these topic areas:

- Belief systems
- Conflict and peace
- Language and communication
- Tradition, culture and identity.

Research information

The following activities will kick-start your thinking about more advanced concepts and help you go beyond the simplistic. You can then plan a line of inquiry based on interesting ideas, opinions, and conclusions. (The sample answers in this section have been written by the author. The way marks are awarded in the real assessment might be different).

Activity 1

(a) What are the key stages of planning a line of inquiry? Refer back to the skills development activities for Section 4 (page 133) to remind yourself.

(b) What strategies have you used previously to help you plan your line of inquiry?

   (i)   Which were most effective?

   (ii)   What improvements do you need to make to your planning and research this time?

   (iii)   How will you make these improvements?

(c) Work in groups to consider questions, key issues, and perspectives on the topic "Belief systems". Ask as many questions as you can think of. Draw diagrams to help you. You could consider some of these questions:

   (i)   How many different kinds of belief can you think of?

   (ii)   What affects our beliefs?

   (iii)   To what extent can we decide what we believe?

Use these questions to help you plan a line of inquiry but you don't need to use them all. You might find it more useful to think deeply about just one or two that interest you rather than find quick and easy answers to all of them.

(iv) Do we have subconscious beliefs that might surprise or even horrify us? If so, how can we combat these beliefs?

(v) Does it matter if we believe different things?

(vi) Are some beliefs wrong and others right, or are they just opinions or perspectives?

(vii) Do any beliefs held by other people upset you? If so, why?

(viii) What links can you see between beliefs, conflict, language, and culture?

(d) Work in groups to consider questions, key issues, and perspectives on the topic "Conflict and peace". Ask as many questions as you can think of. Draw diagrams to help you. You could consider some of these questions:

(i) What is conflict?

(ii) What is peace?

(iii) Is there a right and wrong in most conflicts?

(iv) Conflict drives progress; peace leads to stagnation. Do you agree?

(v) In conflict situations, how important is it to see the other perspective or viewpoint?

(vi) Is it better to negotiate a compromise peacefully or to keep going until you get everything you want? Think about this on the personal, national, and global scales. Is there a difference between toddlers fighting over the best toy, and nations fighting over the best resources?

(vii) How many different ways can you think of to prevent or deal with conflict on personal, national and global scales?

(viii) What is the best way to deal with conflict on the personal, national and global scales?

(ix) What is the best way to prevent conflict on the personal, national and global scales?

(e) Work in groups to consider questions, key issues, and perspectives on the topic Language and communication. Ask as many questions as you can think of. Draw diagrams to help you. You could consider some of these questions:

(i) What is language?

(ii) How does your language affect your thoughts and beliefs?

(iii) Should everyone speak more than one language?

(iv) If you are bilingual, are there some thoughts you can only have in one of your languages? Do you think and behave differently in different languages? For example, some bilingual Chinese–English speakers say they find it easier

to question authority in English than in Chinese, and have more outgoing personalities when they are speaking English. What do you think?

(v) Should there be one world language? If so, which one?

(vi) Is your language a part of your identity?

(vii) Should literature, music, and films be in English to gain a world audience, or in a national language to strengthen local culture?

(viii) Why do young people develop their own forms of language? What purpose do these serve? Should the media use these forms of "yoofspeak"?

(ix) Do you think that lack of communication is the cause of most conflicts? Give your reasons.

(x) Should language adapt to reflect cultural changes or be kept the same to preserve culture?

(f) Working in groups, consider questions, key issues, and perspectives on the topic "Tradition, culture and identity". Ask as many questions as you can think of. Draw diagrams to help you. You could consider some of these questions:

(i) How important are traditions?

(ii) Are traditions just for older people? Should young people develop new ones?

(iii) Are the traditions and culture of your region an important part of your identity? For example, think of a major festival in your country. What would it be like not to celebrate that festival?

(iv) How would you feel about living in a country where your traditions and culture were not important?

(v) How important is it to understand our own traditions?

(vi) How important is it to understand other people's traditions?

(vii) What is culture? Is it art, football, or beliefs? Is it a way of imagining a life different from your own – perhaps by seeing an old church or temple and thinking of the lives of the people who worshipped there, or by seeing the lives of the people in a painting?

(viii) What is a national identity? How does your national identity relate to your personal identity?

(ix) Could we imagine a global identity? What do you think we would need to change for us to see ourselves as citizens of the world?

(g) Choose an issue that interests you and start to plan a line of inquiry.

(i) Remember to consider causes, consequences, possible solutions, and the further consequences of these solutions.

(ii) What search terms will you use?

> **Remember**
>
> It might be more useful to think deeply about one or two questions than to find quick and easy answers to them all.

(h) Which of the following would be good questions for a research report? Explain your answers and improve the questions where necessary.

   (i) Multiculturalism: blessing or curse?

   (ii) How can we create world peace?

   (iii) What measures, if any, should the international community take to promote peace in a region where there is conflict?

   (iv) English: the indispensable language.

   (v) How can a developing country preserve its cultural identity while also joining the world economy?

(i) Work in groups or pairs to think of questions that would be good for a research report.

> **Remember**
>
> Think about how you can improve your search from last time.

Activity 2

The National Film Association of Localia (NFAL) has $1 million to support young film makers and promote the national film industry. The leaders of the NFAL are in conflict about how to spend the money.

A: "What we want to do is support an energetic young producer who will make blockbuster Hollywood-style action movies and really put our film industry on the global map. This will generate the revenue to support even more successful blockbuster movies, and then Localia will become the new Hollywood. We'll all be rich and beautiful, and all our economic problems will be solved."

B: "I think that's utter rubbish! We need to spend less time dreaming about beautiful American actresses and more time thinking about the realities of life in this country."

C: "The world already has Hollywood films. It seems to me that all we could offer would be a poor imitation. We need to do something new and different to captivate audiences."

D: "I agree with you that we shouldn't try to imitate Hollywood. But I don't agree that we need something new. We have our own traditions and our own language. These are being swept away

by American language and values. We should be investing in the development of traditional films, which remind our young people that Localia is important."

B: "What's wrong with American language and values, anyway? And do we want to be stuck in the past, going on about ancient Localian traditions, when we could be making real progress for a modern Localia?"

C: "When I said new, D, I didn't mean completely different from our traditions. I believe that we should support films in Localian, films that emphasize Localian values. But Localia isn't the same place it was when our traditions developed, and I think our values and our films need to develop too. We need a modern vision of our traditions and values – a fusion of old and new."

(a) Identify three types of film that the leaders of NFAL discuss. [3 marks]

(b) Briefly explain what you think B's perspective is. [2 marks]

(c) Summarize the possible advantages and disadvantages of each type of film for Localia. [5 marks]

Question

By now you should be feeling fairly confident about questioning information, ideas, perspectives, and sources independently. Now you are going to extend your ability to question, and practise this skill.

Activity 3

(a) What strategies do you already know for questioning information, ideas, perspectives, and sources? Write a list. Check the skills development activities in Section 1 (pages 1–17), Section 2 (pages 43–62), Section 3 (pages 87–104) and Section 4 (pages 133–156).

(b) What aspects of questioning information, ideas, perspectives, and sources do you need to improve on?

(c) How will you improve this time?

(d) Look over the information, ideas, and sources you found for your research for one of the topics in this section.

    (i) What questions do you need to ask?

    (ii) Do the answers to these questions mean you need to do more research or questioning?

    (iii) What will you do if your sources are unreliable?

> The activities extending your questioning skills are quite advanced, so you may need to go back to previous sections and revise strategies you have already learned before you attempt them. If you can master the activities in this section it will really help your work, so make sure that you have a solid grasp of what you have learned so far.

Beliefs underpinning perspectives

When you consider different perspectives, it can be useful to question the beliefs and values that underlie that perspective. Behaviour that we see and opinions that we hear are based on beliefs, values, and assumptions that we cannot see.

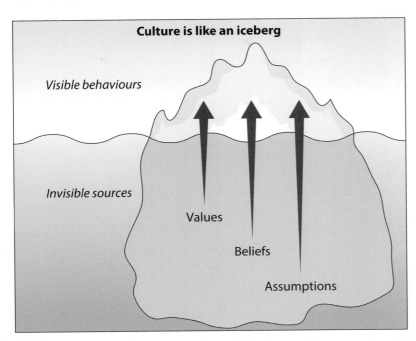

Figure 1 The invisible sources of our behaviour, attitudes, and opinions

In your country:

(a) Are individual rights more important than social stability? If so, why, and if not, why not? What values, beliefs, and assumptions underlie the attitude to individuals and society in your country? Do you agree with these?

(b) Are all people equal? Why (not)? Are young people equal to older people? Why (not)? Should young people respect older people? Why (not)? What values, beliefs, and assumptions underlie the attitude to equality and authority in your country? Do you agree with these?

Examining unspoken beliefs

An action, view, or opinion that makes no sense based on your own values and beliefs can begin to make sense if you understand the beliefs and values that underlie it. Let's look at a simple example:

> Mia is upset because her little brother Amon keeps taking her toys. She thinks that he is being deliberately mean, so she hits him. Amon adores his big sister Mia and wants to share with her. He thinks that whatever she is playing with must be the best toy. He does not understand why she hit him. He feels she is being mean and unfair. Soon there is a big fight, and their mother tells them they are both bad children. They both think this is unfair, and each blames the other. As soon as their mother is not looking, they start fighting again.

Figure 2 How hidden beliefs and values drive behaviour

Let's look at a more complex example.

> Elia is a princess in Ithaca, a world like earth but far, far away. Sapphire, a princess from a neighbouring world, comes to visit. The two make friends and make plans for co-operation between their worlds. Then Elia's father dies, and Elia eats his heart, liver, and brain. Sapphire is disgusted and questions her friendship with Elia. Elia asks what Sapphire would do with her dead. "Bury them, of course," says Sapphire. Elia replies, "Urgh, don't you have any respect for your dead? How could you leave them cold and wasted in the earth? How uncivilized!"

In this situation, Sapphire and Elia need to understand their different values about respecting the dead. In Ithacan culture, eating a relative's organs, and making them a part of you, shows respect and honour. To the Ithacans, burying a dead person seems like abandoning them in an empty void instead of letting them be part of the future. If Sapphire understood this, she would know that her friend was not being disrespectful. She may not be able to overcome her feelings of disgust, but she could use her understanding to counter it, and remain on friendly terms with Elia. If Elia understood the beliefs and values underlying burial of the dead, and realized that it wasn't disrespectful, she would think Sapphire's people less uncivilized.

Activity 5

(a) What do you think their mother could do to help Mia and Amon resolve their conflict?

(b) How much would it help if Mia and Amon understood each other's unspoken beliefs?

(c) What might the consequences be if Princess Elia and Princess Sapphire decide that each other's countries and cultures are uncivilized and savage?

(d) Princess Elia and Princess Sapphire could probably agree to respect each other's values if they understood them, even if they did not share the values.

   (i)   Are there limits to our understanding of other people's values? If so, where are these limits?

   (ii) Work with a partner and explain one of your values to them. Then listen to them explaining one of their values.

(e) Can you think of any examples in our world of misunderstandings based on values?

(f) Think of a conflict happening at the moment. Do you think the different sides are misunderstanding each other's values?

> **(g)** What beliefs and values underlie the following two passages from Activity 2?
>
> **A:** "What we want to do is support an energetic young producer who will make blockbuster Hollywood-style action movies and really put our film industry on the global map. This will generate the revenue to support even more successful blockbuster movies, and then Localia will become the new Hollywood. We'll all be rich and beautiful, and all our economic problems will be solved."
>
> **D:** "…we shouldn't try to imitate Hollywood. But I don't agree that we need something new. We have our own traditions and our own language. These are being swept away by American language and values. We should be investing in the development of traditional films, which remind our young people that Localia is important."

More ways of being illogical

As you have learned, one important way of evaluating the quality of someone's reasoning is to ask: "Is it logical?"

In any argument, always look out for reasoning that isn't logical. Sometimes it is easy to recognize when someone's reasoning is illogical or doesn't make sense. When you are not sure, see whether the argument contains any of the following, which indicate that the reasoning is likely to be illogical:

- Generalizing
- Poor use of facts
- Contradiction and inconsistency
- Not answering someone's argument
- Attacking the arguer, not the argument
- Restricting the options

> If you think someone's reasoning **is** logical, point that out too, and explain why.

Generalizing

Generalizing is moving from a small amount of evidence or from one example to a general claim. For example:

> "That footballer spat in the referee's face. This just shows that all footballers are badly behaved, disrespectful, and a bad influence on young people."

This one example of a footballer behaving badly is used to make a general claim about all footballers. But this is illogical: many footballers do behave well, and we can't judge the behaviour of all footballers from one footballer who is badly behaved.

Poor use of facts

You have learned how important it is to support your opinions with facts and evidence. It is tempting to think that including facts and evidence is enough, but they have to be well used. We have to think about what the facts and evidence really mean. Let's look at two different uses of the same piece of evidence:

> "About 75 per cent of Hindus and Buddhists in America celebrate Christmas. This shows that traditions are completely meaningless and should be abandoned."

Comment: there is no logical connection between the fact given and the conclusion drawn from it. The conclusion is not justified – there is no way that a single statistic could give support to such an extreme conclusion. This is very poor use of evidence.

> "About 75 per cent of Hindus and Buddhists in America celebrate Christmas. They say that it is an opportunity to enjoy time with their own families and to share an experience with their Christian friends. It seems as if sharing celebrations is beneficial, so we could consider encouraging Americans to join in with celebrations such as Diwali."

Comment: This use of the fact is much more thoughtful. By exploring the reasons why Hindus and Buddhists celebrate Christmas, the writer has gained some understanding of what actually underlies the statistic. This allows a more meaningful interpretation of it. In addition, the conclusion here is a suggestion rather than an extreme claim. Of course, you could still argue against the interpretation and the conclusion – but you can't say that it is illogical, like the first example.

Contradiction and inconsistency

Sometimes people contradict themselves in their arguments. Contradiction is saying the direct opposite of what you said before. For example, let's look at two statements made by the same politician to different audiences:

> **Statement 1:** "Every primary-age child should learn a second language because this is the age when you are best able to learn languages."

> **Statement 2:** "We should not be burdening 5-, 6- or 7-year-olds with learning other people's languages. They need to concentrate on mastering their own language at this tender age."

These statements are contradictory. It is not possible that all primary-age children (ages 5–11) should learn a second language if 5- to 7-year-olds should not learn a second language.

Inconsistency occurs when:

- two (or more) things can't both be true at the same time.
- you change your perspective or view without good reason. This is a random sort of change of perspective, which often involves jumping

about without thought. It is different from changing your mind when you've been persuaded by good reasons, or because you are trying to see someone else's point of view.

Let's look at some examples:

Statement 1: "We in Country Y support a peaceful outcome in the conflict between our neighbours, Country X and Country Z."

Statement 2: "Country Y is selling guns to Country X and tanks to Country Z."

Comment: These two statements cannot both be true, so they are logically inconsistent. You could say that it is illogical to claim that both of these statements are true.

Witness 1: "Yes Officer, I saw everything that happened. I was watching very carefully. I clearly saw the white car drive into the back of the red car, just as I was getting my phone out to text my sister."

Witness 2: "I was about the cross the road. The white car was driving along carefully, slowing down to stop at the junction. Then the red car reversed out of a side road, straight into the front of the white car."

Comment: Witness 1 and Witness 2 give contradictory accounts. Saying that the white car drove into the red car is directly opposite to saying that the red car reversed into the white car. Witness 1's account is inconsistent. If the witness was getting their phone out to text, they were presumably looking at the phone for at least some of the time, and not watching carefully.

Not answering someone's argument

When people are having a serious discussion, they often use arguments and explanations to support their views. One really important skill here is answering the other person's arguments and points. Getting this wrong is another way of being illogical. Look out for attempts to answer an argument that are just contradictions or disagreements, or that don't make sense.

Let's look at some different responses to an argument:

Argument: "We should introduce Chinese lessons into schools so that our young people are prepared for the future. China is going to be an increasingly important economic and political power."

Response 1: "No, we should teach Spanish. Spanish is easy to learn."

Comment: Response 1 is just a disagreement, and the point is irrelevant to the economic argument. If we need to learn Chinese for economic reasons, it is illogical to suggest that we should learn Spanish instead just because it's easy.

Response 2: "This would be a good idea, but we might have problems finding enough qualified Chinese teachers."

Comment: Response 2 is more logical. It suggests a practical problem with the proposal put forward in the argument. It does actually answer the argument.

Based on the evidence given, which witness do you think is more reliable? What other questions would you want to ask the witnesses to find out whether they were reliable?

When you are showing that you disagree a different point of view, make sure that you are answering the arguments, not just disagreeing with or ignoring the other person.

Response 3: "The Chinese should learn English."

Comment: Response 3 is merely a disagreement, not an answer to the argument.

Response 4: "Actually, China's economy is declining at the moment, and economic predictions suggest that China will not grow as much or become as economically powerful as we thought. So the case for learning Chinese isn't as strong as all that."

Comment: Response 4 addresses the prediction made in the argument about China's increasing power. It does answer the argument by showing how it might not work if the prediction does not come true. Of course, we can't be sure which prediction is going to come true. So we could argue against this response, but we can't say that it is illogical.

Attacking the arguer, not the argument

Another way of being illogical when you are having a discussion is to attack the person you are arguing against instead of answering their argument. Let's look at an example:

Argument: "We should stop fighting and start negotiating. We have lost too many of our sons, brothers, husbands, and fathers. We are slowly bleeding our nation to death with this war. Our lives and our futures are more important than a small strip of barren land."

Response 1: "We must ignore the bleating of inadequate, fearful pacifists like you and fight our enemies to the death, spilling our blood if need be. We will not be defeated!"

Comment: Response 1 attacks the arguer as "bleating" (like a sheep or goat) and as an "inadequate, fearful pacifist", implying that the argument is based on the other person's fear and cowardice and that we should despise it for that reason. But the response does not address the argument, or show why we should keep fighting. It appeals to our emotions, not our reason, and so this is an illogical response to the argument.

Response 2: "If possible, we should find a solution by negotiation, that's true. But it's not just a strip of barren land we are fighting over. It's a strip of mountain land that not only protects us from invasion but also contains significant mineral wealth. So this bit of land is important to our future, as well as to our people."

Comment: Response 2 answers the points in the argument. It acknowledges that it would be good to negotiate rather than fight, but shows the weak point in the original argument, by saying why the land is important (and therefore perhaps worth fighting for). So this is a logical response – although you could still argue against it. You could question the value that mineral wealth is worth dying for, or you could argue that these mountains clearly don't prevent war, since we're fighting over them…

Restricting the options

When only limited alternatives are considered in an argument and there is at least one additional alternative that is not considered, this can lead to incorrect conclusions. Sometimes called a "false dilemma", restricting the options can often be an attempt to force a choice between two extremes, encouraging "black-or-white thinking". Always consider whether there are other possibilities in an argument that have not been mentioned.

Activity 6

Look again at the discussion in Activity 2 on page 182.

    (a) How effective is A's reasoning?

    (b) How well does B answer the points made by A and D?

    (c) How effective is C's reasoning?

    (d) How effective is D's reasoning?

> **Remember**
>
> Think about the illogical patterns we have considered, but look for other ways of being illogical too. And remember to explain why the reasoning is illogical, if it is.

> "How effective is the reasoning?" means "Does it work well to prove its point?" or "Is it good quality?" Remember to point out the bits that are logical as well as the illogical bits.

Reflect and plan

In this section we have talked about understanding other people's beliefs, values, and assumptions. A related skill is reflecting on what other people must feel, and understanding the world from their perspective. This is called **empathy**. Empathy is an emotional rather than a logical skill – but don't confuse this with emotive or illogical argument. Since one of the aims of Global Perspectives is to "open hearts to the diversity of human experience and feeling", it makes sense to try to understand other people.

Activity 7

There is a civil war in your country. The government is corrupt and only interested in money and power for itself. The opposition started to fight two years ago, hoping for change and a fairer society. But now the opposition has broken down into five different groups who don't agree and there seems to be no prospect of a better future. Your home is rubble, and you have been separated from your family. You do not know if they are still alive.

(a) How do you feel?

(b) What options are available to you? Which one will you choose, and why?

(c) How would you like other people to treat you?

(d) *Either* write a story or poem *or* draw or paint a picture about your situation and your feelings.

> Do people in your country treat refugees the way you would like to be treated?

Activity 8

(a) What skills have you learned to help you reflect on issues and perspectives?

(b) What areas do you still need to improve on?

(c) How are you going to do this?

(d) Look over the research you have done for the topics in this section.

    (i) How have you reflected on the issues and perspectives?

    (ii) How have you changed or developed your own perspectives?

    (iii) How would you help a friend or family member to change or develop their perspective?

(e) Think of a personal situation recently where you disagreed with or did not understand someone. What beliefs, values, assumptions, and feelings might underlie their views and behaviour? What beliefs, values, assumptions, and feelings underlie your own views and behaviour? Are any of these surprising? Can you see how your own underlying perspectives might have influenced the situation? Does understanding these help you deal with the disagreement? If so, how?

(f) Think of an international situation that includes a disagreement or lack of understanding. What beliefs, values, assumptions, and feelings underlie this disagreement? Think about both/ all parties to the conflict.

(g) Use a diagram or mind map to help you reflect on links between the four topics in this section:

- Belief systems
- Conflict and peace
- Tradition, culture and identity
- Language and communication.

(h) How does your personal perspective on these issues link to different local/national and global perspectives?

(i) What is the most important issue that you have considered so far in this section? Why do you think it is the most important?

(j) Can you think of any links between the topics in this section and the other topics that you considered in the previous four sections?

Activity 9

(a) What skills have you learned to help you plan and carry out an active project?

(b) Which of these skills do you need to improve?

(c) How will you improve these skills for your next project?

(d) Which of the following would make good project outcomes for a group of 14–16-year-olds? Explain your answers. Suggest improvements where necessary.

    (a) Make a film about the traditions of an immigrant group in your country.

    (b) Learn a language.

    (c) Work with a group of students from another country to investigate how language, culture, and identity are linked, by learning a bit of each other's language and using this knowledge to considering important aspects of the country's culture and identity.

    (d) Visit a refugee camp and report back to other students and parents.

(e) Work in pairs or groups to think of good project outcomes for a group of 14–16-year-olds.

Present and take action

Activity 10

(a) What skills have you learned for presenting research reports, group projects, and reasoning in an exam? Make a list. Refer back to the skills development activities in Section 1 (pages 1–17), Section 2 (pages 43–62), Section 3 (pages 87–104) and Section 4 (pages 133–156).

(b) Which skills do you most need to improve on?

(c) How will you do this?

(d) Look at a piece of presentation work you have done so far on the course. This might be a spoken presentation, an exam-style argument, or some project documentation.

    (i) How could you improve this piece of work?

    (ii) Actually improve the work – do it again, but better! Look at the difference.

    (iii) Work with a partner on a different piece of presentation work. Make (tactful and positive) suggestions to each other about how you could improve your work.

    (iv) Work together to improve that piece of work.

> When thinking about how you could improve, be precise and focused: "I wrote a list of facts without using them to answer the question. I needed to write an opinion and use the facts to help me support my opinion." Avoid vagueness: "I didn't do the work very well. I didn't try hard enough. I will do better next time."

> Redoing a piece of work is not wasting time. Is Usain Bolt wasting his time when he practises leaving the starting blocks over and over again to get his start as fast as he can?

Using your skills to improve your presentation

When you are developing your own reasoning in research and in examination answers, you can apply the skills you have learned when questioning and reflecting on other people's reasoning. This can help you to write good-quality reasoning, which is logical, empathetic, makes good use of facts and evidence, and which shows that you have really reflected on the issues.

Using evidence

When you include evidence in your reasoning:

- make sure you use it to answer your question
- make your own points and use evidence from different sources to support your points.

Let's look at some examples.

> **A:** "Trevelyan (1992) says that 'tradition is of utmost importance to the preservation of national culture and national self-esteem'. Sivathasen (2012) argues persuasively that 'tradition and culture are such an essential part of any national identity that it is tantamount to a war crime to extinguish local cultural traditions'."

Comment: Two pieces of research have been quoted, but they have not been used to answer a question, and there is no sense of the candidate's own reasoning or views. (NB: the evidence is fabricated for this exercise.)

> **B:** "We should use our money to support local filmmakers who will develop our own traditions and give them new life for the 21st century. This is mostly because our own traditions are important to our nation and we therefore want to support them. **We can see this** in Trevelyan (1992), who says that 'tradition is of utmost importance to the preservation of national culture and national self-esteem'. Sivathasen (2012) **also supports this view,** arguing that 'tradition and culture are [...] an essential part of any national identity'. However, we do not want to live only in the traditions of the past. We want our art to reflect and develop modern life too."

Comment: This is the candidate's own reasoning, and gives a clear sense of their own perspective, supported by evidence, and structured into an argument.

Activity 11

Look at a piece of work you have done already during the course. Choose a piece in which you used a lot of evidence.

(a) Have you used the evidence to answer a question?

(b) Have you provided your own reasoning and supported it with evidence?

(c) Improve the piece of work.

Being logical in your own work

You can identify and explain several ways of being illogical when you see them in other people's reasoning. You need to make sure that you do not become illogical in your own work.

Common ways of students being illogical in research and exams include:

- exaggerating consequences
- generalizing from too little evidence
- forgetting to give reasons, but just stating opinions
- becoming emotional
- answering other viewpoints badly.

Let's look at an example.

> **Answer:** "We should teach our children Chinese. It's really important, otherwise they won't be able to get a job in the future and they'll have no money and their children will starve and our country will sink into economic slump. We should not teach our children Chinese. It's not our language and it's difficult and just imagine all those poor little children in school struggling with that squiggly writing and those strange sounds. They should learn English. It is much easier to learn."

Comment: This is not logical in several ways. The candidate has tried to include two different views, but has not done it well. It looks as if they are contradicting themselves when they say, "We should teach our children Chinese" and "We should not teach our children Chinese." The candidate has also made exaggerated predictions of consequences, and shows emotive reasoning and a lack of understanding of others' views. Is English really easier for Chinese people to learn than Chinese is for English speakers?

Activity 12

(a) Improve the reasoning in the example answer above.

(b) Choose a piece of reasoning you have done. Is it logical? Improve it if you can.

(c) Work with a partner to improve each other's reasoning.

(d) Give a logical response to each of these views:

  (i) We should provide guns to the opposition to help them win the civil war.

  (ii) Our most important priority is developing the economy.

(iii) Everyone ought to speak at least three languages.

(iv) Our national identity is more important than international links.

(v) Democracy is the only acceptable form of government.

(e) Working in pairs or small groups, play "Argument tennis". Person/team 1 makes a claim, person/team 2 argues against it, person/team 1 argues back again. Keep going as long as possible. The last person or team to argue without repetition wins.

Using reflection in your reasoning

If you have reflected on a topic, this will show in your reasoning. Using reflection will enable you to:

- go beyond the source material, expressing personal thoughts on what the material means or implies
- come up with your own arguments and ideas, as well as using ideas from source material
- have a personal perspective that makes sense and is based on the evidence
- suggest compromises between different views or perspectives.

Let's look at an example of two students writing about the situation in Activity 2:

Student 1: "One option is to fund Hollywood-style action movies. This could address a world market and bring much-needed money to Localia. On the other hand, it would not preserve local traditions. Another option is to fund films in a local tradition. This would preserve local culture, but would not speak to a world market. There are enough Hollywood-style movies in the world anyway, so I think that NFAL should fund films in a local tradition."

Comment: This student has analysed two of the options quite well, and made good use of the material in the source. They have avoided the illogical reasoning in the source and summed up the advantages and disadvantages of the two options. This is a reasonable response, but contains no new thoughts and little evidence of reflection.

Student 2: "The NFAL could try to fund a movie with Hollywood-type appeal, but also with a local identity. This would merge the two desires to make films that make money in the global market and to make films that remind young people that local traditions and values are important. However, this attempt might not succeed. This is because you need to care about an issue and a story to make a good movie. Looking for a formula to make a 'successful' movie seems to me to be missing the important aspects that do make a good movie. For this reason I believe that the NFAL should stop worrying about tradition and fund a filmmaker with passion and talent, who sees good stories with real human interest."

Comment: This student has really considered the issue, and has developed a clear and thoughtful personal perspective. The student has proposed two possible solutions that were not made in the stimulus material, and reasoned about them. They have also thought about what qualities a good film should have. This is not a perfect answer – it would be nice to see more thinking about the value of tradition – but it does clearly show reflection.

Activity 13

(a) How do you think the NFAL from Activity 2 should spend their money (promoting the Localian film industry)? In your answer, you should:

- state your conclusion
- give reasons and examples
- consider at least one other view.

(b) Are traditions just for older people? In your answer, you should:

- state your conclusion
- give reasons and examples
- consider at least one other view.

Section 5
17 Belief systems

Individual research

Activity 17.1

(a) Remind yourself of the key stages of planning an inquiry.

(b) Choose an issue relating to belief systems that interests you.

(c) Set a question.

(d) Research, question, and reflect.

(e) Remind yourself of the precise assessment requirements for a research report.

    (i) Remember to consider a problem, its causes and consequences, different perspectives, possible solutions, and the consequences of these possible solutions.

    (ii) Remember that you need to develop a line of reasoning – using your research to help you support a conclusion, decision, or proposal for action.

(f) Write your research report.

> You can choose your own question, but here are some suggestions:
>
> - How can we encourage people to respect each other's beliefs in a multicultural society?
>
> - How important is the role of belief in modern society?

Remember

A good question will:

▶ give you focus

▶ require you to develop a line of reasoning (this means justifying opinions and values, not just describing)

▶ help you meet the assessment requirements, including looking at problems, their causes and consequences, possible solutions, and different perspectives.

Look back at the feedback you received on previous research reports. What do you need to improve on? How will you improve it this time?

Group project

Activity 17.2

(a) Form a group and remind yourselves of the key stages in planning, managing, and carrying out a project.

(b) Discuss with your teacher how you can collaborate with people from another country or culture.

(c) Set an outcome.

(d) Remind yourselves of the precise assessment criteria for a group project.

(e) Plan, manage, and carry out your project.

(f) Evaluate your project.

> You can choose your own project outcome, but here are some suggestions:
>
> ● Organize an interfaith activity in your community.
>
> ● Work with students from a different culture to complete a display comparing your different beliefs (about society, authority, customs…).

Is your outcome SMART?

Look back at previous self-evaluations. What do you need to improve on? How can you improve this time?

Remember

Always respect other people's beliefs, even if you disagree with them.

Written exam practice

Document 1

Image 1

Image 2

Figure 17.1 Cartoons about belief

"There are two ways to be fooled. One is to believe what isn't true; the other is to refuse to believe what is true." **Kierkegaard**

"Faith is the great cop-out, the great excuse to evade the need to think and evaluate evidence. Faith is belief in spite of, even perhaps because of, the lack of evidence." **Richard Dawkins**

"I believe that even amid today's mortar bursts and whining bullets, there is still hope for a brighter tomorrow... I have the audacity to believe that peoples everywhere can have three meals a day for their bodies, education and culture for their minds, and dignity, equality and freedom for their spirits." **Martin Luther King Jr**

Source: http://www.nobelprize.org/nobel_prizes/peace/laureates/1964/king-acceptance_en.html

Document 2

The placebo effect

The placebo effect is well known in medicine. It happens when a patient thinks that they have been given medication, but this is actually a pill with no medical benefits (a **placebo**). The patient gets better because they believe they are being healed.

In a recent study, different groups were given different information about the effects of an energy drink on mental performance. They were then asked to drink the drink and attempt a word test. Here are the results:

Group	Information given about the drink	Score
Control group	No information given	7 words
Group 1	The drink provides a slight improvement to mental performance.	5–6 words
Group 2	The drink provides a slight improvement, and was bought at a discount for $0.89	4 words
Group 3	The drink provides a significant improvement to mental performance.	8–9 words
Group 4	The drink provides a significant improvement to mental performance and was bought at the full price of $1.89.	10 + words

Document 3

How far should we tolerate other people's beliefs? The answer here is not simple. Our behaviour depends on our beliefs. We clean our teeth because we believe that will keep them healthy. We look after family members because we believe it is right to do so. We act because of our beliefs about religion. And our beliefs affect the way we react to other people.

This means that beliefs are not entirely private. For example, if someone is preaching hatred and violence against other people, this is a public matter. Their beliefs affect me if it leads to violence in my neighbourhood. So I have the right to object to their beliefs.

But where do we draw the line between tolerance and intolerance? For me, we shouldn't tolerate beliefs that cause harm. Beliefs can cause harm by promoting or justifying harm towards others, or even just by stopping people thinking about the world with an open mind.

@deepthinker: "This is fine, but you're confusing belief and action. It's the action of preaching hatred and violence that causes harm."

@Suki: "This is all very well, but can we agree on harm? Let's say my beliefs about motherhood lead me to report a mother for leaving her tiny children alone while she goes out. The children are taken from the mother. Have my beliefs led me to do good or harm?"

@thatsallthereis: "You're all wishy-washy liberals who should just keep quiet. You've nothing to say. The facts are simple: either we tolerate all beliefs, or we tolerate none. Then we would descend into a tyranny of the mind, where there can be no freedom. This would lead to the loss of everything we believe in – all political advances, scientific progress, and technological breakthroughs."

Question 1

(a) Identify three different kinds of belief dealt with in
   Documents 1 to 3.   [3 marks]

(b) Look at Figure 17.1. Why might there be a conflict between
   intellectual integrity and belief? Explain your answer.   [3 marks]

(c) Look at Document 2. Explain how different beliefs about
   the energy drink affected people's performance in the
   word test.   [3 marks]

(d) Is belief just a personal issue? Briefly justify your answer
   with reference to national and global perspectives.   [3 marks]

Question 2

(a) Look at the study described in Document 2. What additional information would you need in order to decide whether the drink itself has an effect on mental performance? How would this information help you? **[3 marks]**

Piece of information:	
How it would help:	

(b) In Document 3, **@Suki** asks, "Have my beliefs led me to do good or harm?" What additional information would you need about the situation in order to answer this question? How would this information help you decide whether **@Suki**'s beliefs led her to do good or harm? **[9 marks]**

> Consider the differences between **(a)** and **(b)**. Part **(a)** is a 3-mark question, and part **(a)** is a 9-mark question. How do you think the answers should be different?

Question 3

All questions relate to Document 3.

(a) "Our behaviour depends on our beliefs."
Is this a fact or an opinion? Justify your answer. **[3 marks]**

(b) "We shouldn't tolerate beliefs that cause harm."
Is this a fact, an opinion, a value judgment, or a prediction, or more than one of these? Justify your answer. **[3 marks]**

(c) Is cleaning our teeth a good example of how beliefs affect our behaviour? Explain your answer. **[3 marks]**

(d) How reasonable is **@deepthinker**'s response to the article? Justify your answer. **[3 marks]**

(e) How effective is the reasoning provided by **@thatsallthereis**? Justify your answer. **[6 marks]**

> "How effective is the reasoning?" is another way of asking, "Is the reasoning good quality?" or "Does the reasoning work well?"

Question 4

How far should we tolerate other people's beliefs? **[18 marks]**

In your answer you should:

● state your conclusion

● give your reasons for it

● give examples, where relevant

● show that you have considered at least one other viewpoint.

Section 5
18 Conflict and peace

Individual research

Activity 18.1

(a) Remind yourself of the key stages of planning an inquiry.

(b) Choose an issue relating to conflict and peace that interests you.

(c) Set a question.

(d) Research, question, and reflect.

(e) Remind yourself of the precise assessment requirements for a research report.

    (i) Remember to consider a problem, its causes and consequences, different perspectives, possible solutions, and the consequences of these possible solutions.

    (ii) Remember that you need to develop a line of reasoning – using your research to help you support a conclusion, decision, or proposal for action.

(f) Write your research report.

> You can choose your own question, but here are some suggestions:
>
> • Choose a particular conflict. What are the causes and consequences of this conflict and how could peace be achieved in the conflict?
>
> • How effective is the UN as a peacekeeper?

Group project

Written exam practice

Document 1

Two people who saw this martial arts leaflet in college had a discussion:

Nick: "Everyone knows it's a really bad idea to teach people how to be violent. It's like sending aggressive young men into the army and teaching them to use guns. It's just asking for trouble in our streets. It'll lead to civil war and the end of civilized society."

Katie: "I disagree. I think martial arts are really good because they teach people focus and concentration and respect for others. These things are really important for education. So a lot of young kids can do better at school because of the skills they learn at a martial art."

Nick: "What do you know? You're just a girl. It's so obviously wrong to teach people skills that they can use to hurt other people with. They should all be banned."

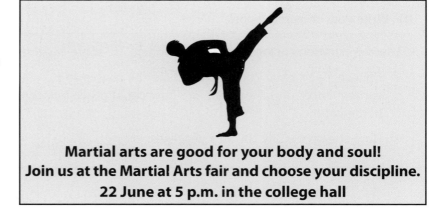

Martial arts are good for your body and soul!
Join us at the Martial Arts fair and choose your discipline.
22 June at 5 p.m. in the college hall

Figure 18.1 A leaflet advertising martial arts

Katie: "So, you couldn't hurt anyone with the skills you use to kick a football? Should we ban that too? I've seen more undisciplined fights on the football field than among people who do martial arts. And what do I know? Well, I'm a qualified Tae Kwon Do youth leader. I got my black belt when I was ten. I'm only one example, but kicking and punching pads helps me to get rid of my frustrations after a bad day, and we do patterns and exercises to focus the mind."

Nick: "You're just not listening. It's wrong, I tell you."

Nick goes red in the face and grabs Katie. Katie puts Nick on the floor.

Katie: "A martial art can teach women vital skills like self-defence. And because it also teaches self-control, I haven't actually hurt you."

Document 2

Conflictia: a troubled country

Conflictia is a country that has experienced three decades of political unrest, changing governments, and civil wars. To understand why, it helps to know about its history.

Until the 1800s, Conflictia had a population of traditional tribes, which followed traditional religions, and Muslims who had migrated to Conflictia. From the 1820s to the 1840s, former US slaves settled in Conflictia; many of these settlers believed their ancestors had originally come from Conflictia.

The settlers "bought" land from the tribes, but failed to understand that the tribes believed that the land belonged to everyone, and that it could not be owned and passed down through one family. The settlers also established a constitution and a set of laws, but they did not recognize the traditional tribes as citizens. Over time, this created economic and social differences between the groups, and much resentment.

Over the years, a number of different ethnic groups from other countries in the region migrated to Conflictia. Some of these people were fleeing from wars, famine, and poverty. As a result, by the 1980s, Conflictia had several ethnic and religious groups, with different identities characterized by different levels of economic and political power, different languages, dress styles, family systems, land ownership, and education.

Incompetent and corrupt governments used the money from natural resources such as diamonds to fund luxurious lifestyles. Eventually, the different ethnic and religious groups began fighting to gain control of the country, and they started to blame one another for the conflict. Money from diamonds was now used to fund warfare. Foreign powers donated $500 million to support one military power or another.

As the institutions of the state disintegrated, poverty increased. Fighting in the civil wars became the largest employment opportunity. Child soldiers became adult soldiers who could not remember peace.

Question 1

Consider Document 1.

(a) Identify three benefits of learning a martial art. [3 marks]

Consider Document 2.

(b) Outline the causes and consequences that led to civil war in Conflictia. Use a diagram or flow chart to help you. [9 marks]

Question 2

(a) You want to find out whether Nick or Katie is right about the effects of learning a martial art.

    (i) What sort of evidence would help you decide whether Nick or Katie is right? [3 marks]

    (ii) What problems would you expect to have in researching this evidence? [3 marks]

(b) You need to establish how bad the humanitarian crisis is in Conflictia.

    (i) How would you research evidence? [3 marks]

    (ii) What problems would you expect to have in researching this evidence? [3 marks]

Question 3

(a) A refugee from Conflictia tells you: "The only way to help Conflictia is by supporting the Conflictian Liberation Army (CLA). The CLA will bring peace and unity to the people, and we need guns and tanks and nuclear missiles to achieve this peace. I know; I've been there."

    (i) Do you think this refugee would provide reliable knowledge claims? Explain your answer. [3 marks]

    (ii) How logical is this refugee's reasoning? Justify your answer. [3 marks]

> "How effective is the reasoning?" is another way of asking, "Is the reasoning good quality?" or "Does the reasoning work well?"

(b) Whose reasoning is more effective, Nick's or Katie's? Explain your answer.

In your answer, you may consider some of the following:

- The reliability of their knowledge claims
- How logical they are
- How reasonable any causes or consequences they suggest are
- How well they answer each other's points
- Any other relevant issues [12 marks]

Question 4

You have to advise your government on the appropriate action for your country to take regarding Conflictia. Options for your country include (but are not limited to) the following:

- Fund one group so that there is one victor who can form an unchallenged government.
- Support UN peacekeeping troops.
- Send your own army.
- Work with local economic and religious organizations.
- Provide a "neutral space" for negotiation to achieve an agreed peace.
- Work with local organizations to provide therapy, education, and support for economic growth.
- Provide humanitarian aid.

Write a proposal supporting one or more actions.   [18 marks]

In your answer you should:

- state your conclusion
- give your reasons for it
- give examples, where relevant
- show that you have considered at least one other viewpoint.

Section 5

19 Language and communication

Individual research

Activity 19.1

(a) Remind yourself of the key stages of planning an inquiry.

(b) Choose an issue relating to language and communication that interests you.

(c) Set a question.

(d) Research, question, and reflect.

(e) Remind yourself of the precise assessment requirements for a research report.

    (i) Remember to consider a problem, its causes and consequences, different perspectives, possible solutions, and the consequences of these possible solutions.

    (ii) Remember that you need to develop a line of reasoning – using your research to help you support a conclusion, decision, or proposal for action.

(f) Write your research report.

> You can choose your own question, but here are some suggestions:
>
> ● How can we keep endangered languages alive (and should we)?
>
> ● How important is language to culture and identity?

Remember

A good question will:

▶ give you focus

▶ require you to develop a line of reasoning (this means justifying opinions and values, not just describing)

▶ help you meet the assessment requirements, including looking at problems, their causes and consequences, possible solutions, and different perspectives.

Look back at the feedback you received on previous research reports. What do you need to improve on? How will you improve it this time?

Group project

Activity 19.2

(a) Form a group and remind yourselves of the key stages in planning, managing, and carrying out a project.

(b) Discuss with your teacher how you can collaborate with people from another country or culture.

(c) Set an outcome.

(d) Remind yourselves of the precise assessment criteria for a group project.

(e) Plan, manage, and carry out your project.

(f) Evaluate your project.

You can choose your own project outcome, but here are some suggestions:

- If you live in a multicultural area, work with members of different cultural groups. Organize regular language classes so that you learn each other's languages. Produce a short, multilingual video with English subtitles, showing your progress. Alternatively, produce a short video in the other language and explain how you have benefited from learning it.

- Work with students from a different culture to complete a video or leaflet showing how your different languages affect your identities.

Is your outcome SMART?

Look back at previous self-evaluations. What do you need to improve on? How can you improve this time?

Remember

Always respect other people's traditions and cultures.

Written exam practice

Document 1

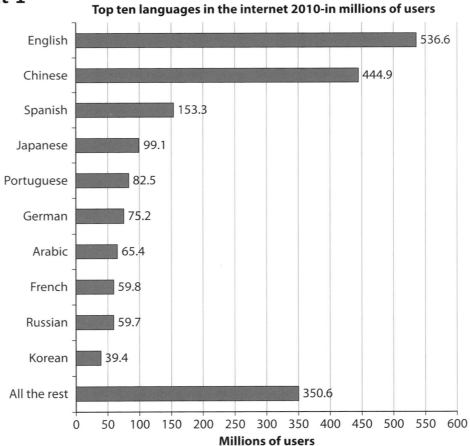

Top ten languages in the internet 2010-in millions of users

Language	Millions of users
English	536.6
Chinese	444.9
Spanish	153.3
Japanese	99.1
Portuguese	82.5
German	75.2
Arabic	65.4
French	59.8
Russian	59.7
Korean	39.4
All the rest	350.6

Source: Internet World Stats-www.internetworldstats.com/stats7.htm
Estimated internet users are 1, 966, 514, 816 on June 30, 2010
Copyright© 2000-2010, Miniwatts Marketing Group

Figure 19.1 The top ten languages used on the Internet, 2010

Document 2

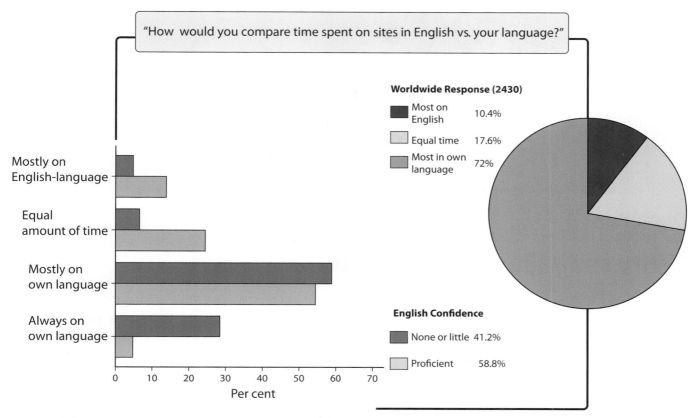

"How would you compare time spent on sites in English vs. your language?"

Worldwide Response (2430)

Most on English	10.4%
Equal time	17.6%
Most in own language	72%

English Confidence

None or little	41.2%
Proficient	58.8%

Mostly on English-language

Equal amount of time

Mostly on own language

Always on own language

Per cent

Figure 19.2 How non-Anglophone consumers use English-language websites

We surveyed over 2,400 consumers from eight non-Anglophone countries: Brazil, China, France, Germany, Japan, Russia, Spain, and Turkey.

Source: "Can't Read, Won't Buy," Common Sense Advisory research, www.commonsenseadvisory.com

Document 3

Modern English Lesson by Eric Per1in

The word "said" is now considered outmoded and officially archaic. In modern English, the proper phrase is "was like."

INCORRECT:
Bill said, "How are you?" and Jill said, "I'm fine."

CORRECT:
Bill was like, "How are you?" and Jill was like, "I'm fine."

www.funnytimes.com

Figure 19.3 "Modern English lesson" by Eric Perlin

Figure 19.4 "Modern languages"

"Son, we're learning how to speak teenage."

Document 4

Why sexist language matters

In my work on gender equality, I focus on words that students consider just fine: male (so-called) generics. Some of these words refer to persons occupying a position: postman, chairman, freshman, congressman, fireman. Other words refer to the entire universe of human beings: "mankind" or "he." Then we've got manpower, manmade lakes and "Oh, man, where did I leave my keys?" There's "manning" the tables in a country where children learn that "all men are created equal". The worst, from my observations, is the popular expression "you guys". Please don't tell me it's a regional term. I've heard it in the Triangle, New York, Chicago, San Francisco and Montreal. I've seen it in print in national magazines, newsletters and books. And even if it were regional, that doesn't make it right. I'll bet we can all think of a lot of practices in our home regions that we'd like to get rid of.

I sound defensive. I know. But that's because I've so often heard (and not only from students) … *What's the big deal?*

One consequence of male-based generics is that they reinforce the system in which "man" in the abstract and men in the flesh are privileged over women. But the words we use can also reinforce current realities when they are sexist (or racist). Words are tools of thought. We can use words to maintain the status quo *or* to think in new ways – which in turn creates the possibility of a new *reality*. It makes a difference if I think of myself as a "girl" or a "woman"; it makes a difference if we talk about "Negroes" or "African–Americans". Do we want a truly inclusive language or one that just pretends?

In 1986 Douglas Hofstadter, a philosopher, wrote a parody of sexist language by making an analogy with race. His article ("A Person Paper on Purity in Language") creates an imaginary world in which generics are based on race rather than gender. In that world, people would use "fresh *white*," "chair *white*" and yes, "you *whiteys*." People of color would hear "all whites are created equal" – and be expected to feel included. Substituting "white" for "man" makes it easy to see why using "man" for all human beings is wrong. Yet, women are expected to feel flattered by "freshman", "chairman" and "you guys".

And can you think of one, just one, example of a female-based generic? Try using "freshwoman" with a group of male students or calling your male boss "chairwoman". Then again, don't. There could be serious consequences for referring to a man as a "woman" – a term that still means "lesser" in our society. If not, why do men get so upset at the idea of being called women?

Sherryl Kleinman teaches in the Department of Sociology at the University of North Carolina

Source: http://www.alternet.org/story/48856/why_sexist_language_matters

Question 1

(a) Look at the statistics in Documents 1 and 2. Do the statistics give you good reason to accept the claim that "all companies should have English and Chinese versions of their website"? Justify your answer. [3 marks]

(b) Choose one cartoon from Document 3 and explain the issue it raises with regard to language. Consider causes, consequences, and different perspectives on the issue. [9 marks]

Question 2

(a) What information do you need to help you explain the statistics in Document 1? How would this information help to explain the statistics? [9 marks]

(b) How exactly would you find this information? [3 marks]

Question 3

Consider Document 4.

(a) Is Sherryl Kleinman a reliable source of information on gender equality and language? Justify your answer. [3 marks]

(b) Is this article mostly fact or opinion? Justify your answer. [3 marks]

(c) How effective is Kleinman's reasoning? [12 marks]

> "How effective is the reasoning?" is another way of asking, "Is the reasoning good quality?" or "Does the reasoning work well?"

In your answer you should consider:

- the causes and consequences she suggests

- whether you agree with any of the values she expresses

- any other relevant issues.

Question 4

How important is it to have one standard form of a language? [18 marks]

In your answer you should:

- state your conclusion

- give your reasons for it

- give examples, where relevant

- show that you have considered at least one other viewpoint.

> You could consider the effects of teenage languages, regional dialects, and international variations such as US English, British English, Australian English, Chinglish, Singlish...

Section 5
20 Tradition, culture and identity

Your individual research

Activity 20.1

(a) Remind yourself of the key stages of planning an inquiry.

(b) Choose an issue relating to tradition, culture and identity that interests you.

(c) Set a question.

(d) Research, question and reflect.

(e) Remind yourself of the precise assessment requirements for a research report.

    (i) Remember to consider a problem, its causes and consequences, different perspectives, possible solutions, and the consequences of these possible solutions.

    (ii) Remember that you need to develop a line of reasoning – using your research to help you support a conclusion, decision, or proposal for action.

(f) Write your research report.

> You can choose your own question, but here are some suggestions:
>
> ● How can we develop a valuable national identity while also respecting the cultural identities of immigrants?
>
> ● How important are tradition and culture to our identity in modern society?
>
> ● Football – our best hope for a global culture?

Look back at the feedback you received on previous research reports. What do you need to improve on? How will you improve it this time?

Your group project

Activity 20.2

(a) Form a group and remind yourselves of the key stages in planning, managing, and carrying out a project.

(b) Discuss with your teacher how you can collaborate with people from another country or culture.

(c) Set an outcome.

(d) Remind yourselves of the precise assessment criteria for a group project.

(e) Plan, manage, and carry out your project.

(f) Evaluate your project.

You can choose your own project outcome, but here are some suggestions:

- If you live in a multicultural area, work with members of different cultural groups. Organize an event celebrating different traditions and cultures. Produce information leaflets for visitors to increase their understanding.

- Work with students from a different culture to complete a display comparing your different traditions and how these affect your identities.

Is your outcome SMART?

Look back at previous self-evaluations. What do you need to improve on? How can you improve this time?

Remember

Always respect other people's traditions and cultures in your work.

Written exam practice

Document 1

"Preservation of one's own culture does not require contempt or disrespect for other cultures." **Cesar Chavez**

"No two languages are ever sufficiently similar to be considered as representing the same social reality. The worlds in which different societies live are distinct worlds, not merely the same world with different labels attached." **Amy Tan**

"We are in the process of creating what deserves to be called the idiot culture. Not an idiot sub-culture, which every society has bubbling beneath the surface and which can provide harmless fun; but the culture itself. For the first time, the weird and the stupid and the coarse are becoming our cultural norm, even our cultural ideal." **Carl Bernstein**

"I dreamt last night that a lecture about the decline of culture in the early twenty-first century topped the viewing figures on YouTube."

Figure 20.1 The decline of culture?

Document 2

Cultural identity in New Zealand: a social report

For many people, television is a major source of news, information, and entertainment and it strongly influences their sense of local and national identity. A local content measure reflects the extent to which we see our culture reflected through this medium.

In 2009, local content on six national free-to-air television channels made up 39 per cent of the prime-time schedule.

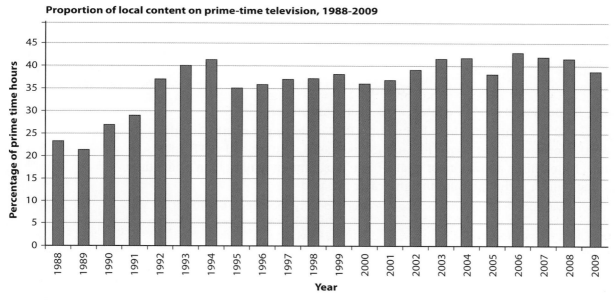

Proportion of local content on prime-time television, 1988-2009

Source: NZ On Air
Notes: (1) Up to 2004, the figures are for prime-time (6pm –10pm local content on TV One, TV2 and TV3 only. (2) Figures from 2005 include Prime Television and Māori Televison (2005 Māori Televison figure derived by the Ministry of Social Development). (3) Figures from 2006 include C4.

Figure 20.2 Proportion of local content on prime-time TV in New Zealand, 1988–2009

The percentage of local content in prime-time transmission hours in 2009 differs across the channels: TV One: 51 per cent, TV2: 20 per cent, TV3: 44 per cent, Prime: 13 per cent, Māori Television: 54 per cent, and C4: 53 per cent.

International comparisons are difficult due to the inconsistencies in measurement approaches by different countries. However, in 1999, local content accounted for 38 per cent of total transmission time in New Zealand, a smaller proportion than that in 10 other surveyed countries.

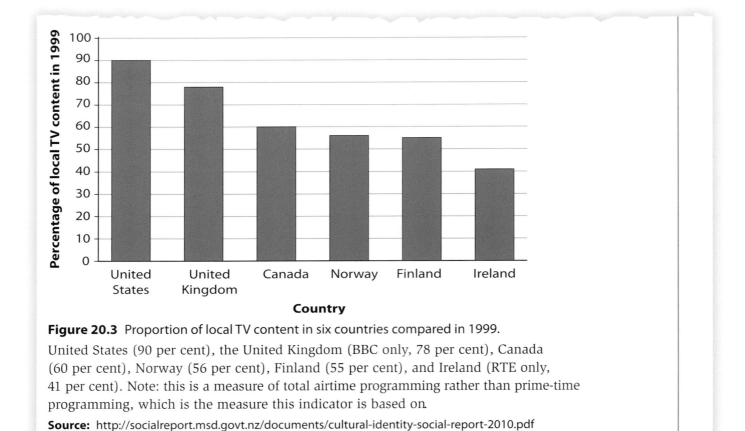

Figure 20.3 Proportion of local TV content in six countries compared in 1999.
United States (90 per cent), the United Kingdom (BBC only, 78 per cent), Canada
(60 per cent), Norway (56 per cent), Finland (55 per cent), and Ireland (RTE only,
41 per cent). Note: this is a measure of total airtime programming rather than prime-time
programming, which is the measure this indicator is based on.

Source: http://socialreport.msd.govt.nz/documents/cultural-identity-social-report-2010.pdf

Document 3

@anti_globalization: "We have to fight globalization or it will bring about the end of everything we value. It's destroying our local cultural identities and making us all the same. We all watch American TV, eat burgers and buy our clothes at the same chain stores. You can walk through Shanghai, New York, London, or Delhi and not know which city or even which continent you're in. The only differences are fakes of local traditions put there for tourists."

@global_girl: "Shopping and tourist districts aren't exactly culture, are they? If @anti_globalization ever got beyond the tourist districts, he would notice the real cities with their own distinct identities!"

@lovemynationbecauseimtoldto: "What is cultural identity anyway? Isn't it just another Western idea that we all have to accept? Governments and the media put a lot of effort into creating national identities and they tell us we have to accept them or be 'unpatriotic'. But actually, lots of these nations traditionally have many shifting cultural groups. There isn't just one, national, traditional identity that never changed until globalization. These are just social constructs. And they're breaking down in many places – look at Wales and Scotland breaking away from England, or civil war in Syria, or … you could name anywhere in the world and find national identities breaking down because they were never real."

@global_girl: "Well, **@lovemynationbecauseimtoldto** has one good point. Identity isn't a fixed thing. I'm Chinese when I'm with my mother's parents, but Indian when I'm with my father's parents, and Australian when I'm with my friends. All these things are who I am, but none of them is all of me."

Question 1

(a) Identify and explain two different understandings of culture from Document 1.　　　　　　　　　[6 marks]

(b) Do you think that culture is mostly a personal, local/national or global issue? Justify your answer. You may refer to any of the documents and/or to your own knowledge.　　[6 marks]

Question 2

(a) Document 2 states: "A local content measure reflects the extent to which we see our culture reflected through [TV]." What do you need to know about the types of programme shown on New Zealand TV to decide whether it really is showing local culture?　　　　　　　　　[6 marks]

What I need to know:	
How it will help me decide:	

(b) According to Document 2, in 1999, television in the UK (BBC only) showed 78 per cent local content. What else do you need to know to decide whether television in the UK strongly reflects local culture?　　　　　[6 marks]

What I need to know:	
How it will help me decide:	

Question 3

(a) Is a social report produced by the New Zealand government a reliable source of information? Justify your answer.　　[3 marks]

(b) Why might it be problematic to compare total air-time programming with prime-time programming? Justify your answer.　　　　　　　　　　　[3 marks]

(c) Whose reasoning is most effective – **@anti_globalization's**, **@global_girl's** or **@lovemynationbecauseimtoldto's?**

In your answer, consider some of the following:

- The reliability of any knowledge claims they make
- How logical their reasoning is
- How well they answer each other's points
- Whether you agree with any values they express
- Any other relevant points　　　　　　[12 marks]

> "How effective is the reasoning?" is another way of asking, "Is the reasoning good quality?" or "Does the reasoning work well?"

Question 4

What are the most important aspects of culture, in your opinion?

[18 marks]

In your answer you should:

- state your conclusion
- give your reasons for it
- give examples, where relevant
- show that you have considered at least one other viewpoint.

You could consider aspects of culture such as art, sport, architecture, traditions, language, religion, festivals, attitudes and beliefs, food, shopping, or fashion.